111	×2 cards		127	number cards (5
112	×2, ×5, ×10 cards		128	number cards (6
113	stamps		129	number cards (8
114	number game		130	tens cards
115	quartering cards		131	2D shape cards
116	pegboard game		132	more 2D shape
117	squares		133	2D shape vocabulary
118	tocker rocker		134	3D shape vocabulary
119	digital clock sheet		135	faces vocabulary
120	time dominoes		136	day cards
121	more time dominoes		137	length vocabulary
122	counting objects		138	mass vocabulary
123	Peter Piper		139	capacity vocabulary
124	counting sheet		140	cm-square grid
125	number cards (21–36)		141	seasons cards
126	number cards (37–52)			

1 Name ....

1	2	3	4	5	6	7	8	9	10
11	12	13	14	15	16	17	18	19	20
21	22	23	24	25	26	27	28	29	30
31	32	33	34	35	36	37	38	39	40
41	42	43	44	45	46	47	48	49	50
51	52	53	54	55	56	57	58	59	60
61	62	63	64	65	66	67	68	69	70
71	72	73	74	75	76	77	78	79	80
81	82	83	84	85	86	87	88	89	90
91	92	93	94	95	96	97	98	99	100

2   Name ....

1	2	3	4	5	6	7	8	9	10
36	37	38	39	40	41	42	43	44	11
35	64	65	66	67	68	69	70	45	12
34	63	84	85	86	87	88	71	46	13
33	62	83	96	97	98	89	72	47	14
32	61	82	95	100	99	90	73	48	15
31	60	81	94	93	92	91	74	49	16
30	59	80	79	78	77	76	75	50	17
29	58	57	56	55	54	53	52	51	18
28	27	26	25	24	23	22	21	20	19

3 Name

Numeracy Focus 2: Games and Activity Support Sheets

4 Name

Numeracy Focus 2: Games and Activity Support Sheets

© P. Latham, H. Williams, M. Askew and S. Ebbutt 2001. Rigby
For copyright restrictions see reverse of title page.

5 Name ....

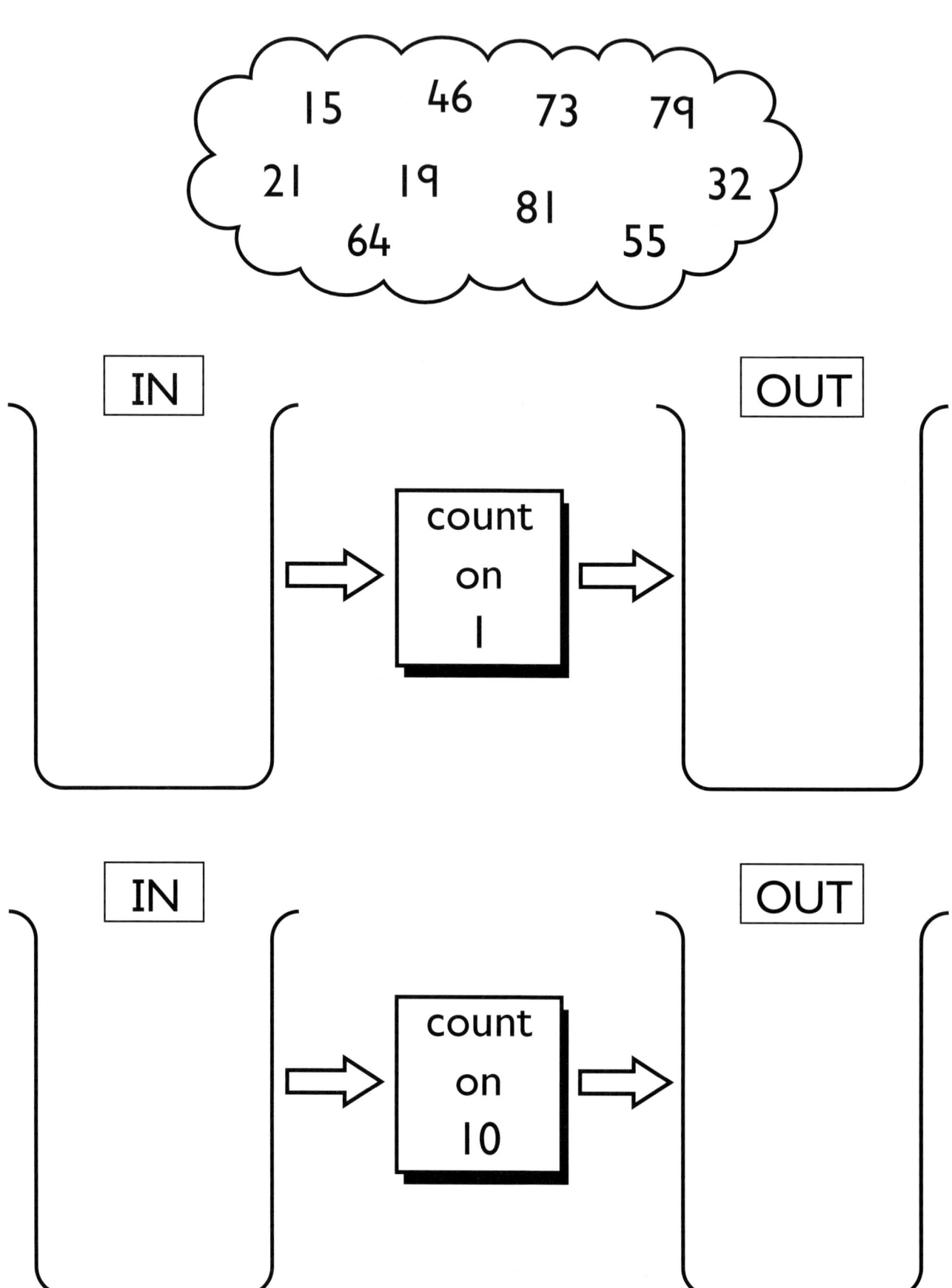

Count in ones

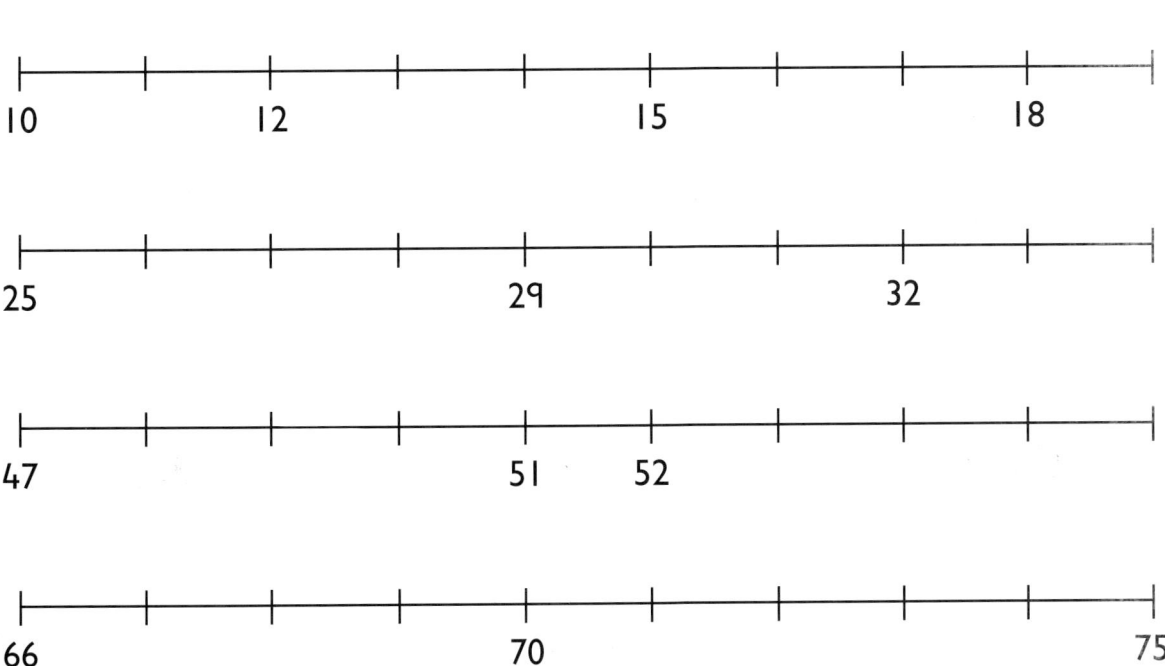

Count in tens

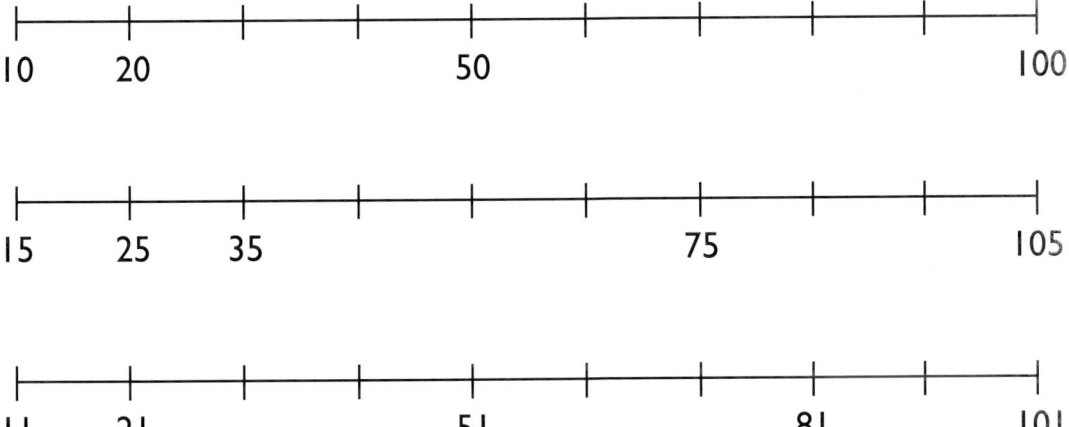

7 Name ....

1p	2p
3p	4p
5p	6p
7p	8p
9p	10p

Numeracy Focus 2: Games and Activity Support Sheets

8 Name ....

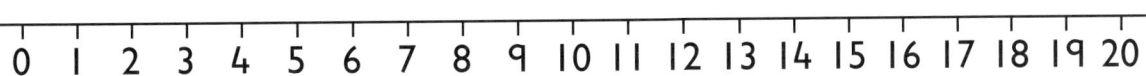

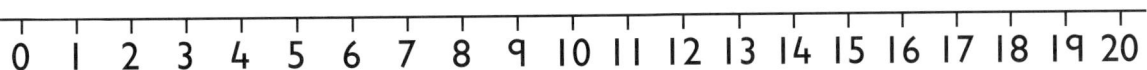

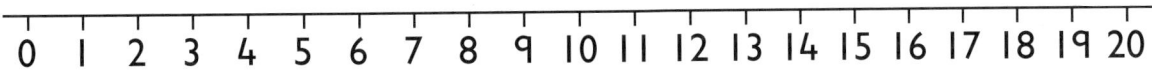

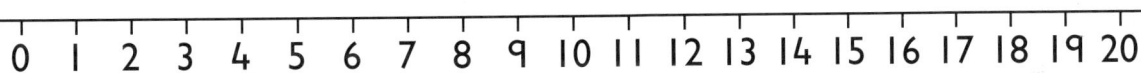

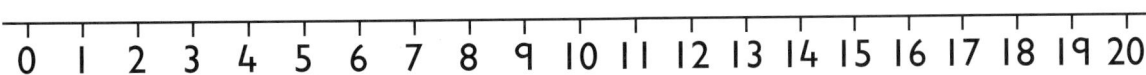

9 Name _____

January	January	February	February
March	March	April	April
May	May	June	June
July	July	August	August
September	September	October	October
November	November	December	December

0	1	2	3	4
5	6	7	8	9
10	11	12	13	14
15	16	17	18	19
20	21	22	23	24
25	26	27	28	29

11 Name ....

1	2	3	4	5	6	7	8	9	10
11	12	13	14	15	16	17	18	19	20
21	22	23	24	25	26	27	28	29	30
31	32	33	34	35	36	37	38	39	40
41	42	43	44	45	46	47	48	49	50
51	52	53	54	55	56	57	58	59	60
61	62	63	64	65	66	67	68	69	70
71	72	73	74	75	76	77	78	79	80
81	82	83	84	85	86	87	88	89	90
91	92	93	94	95	96	97	98	99	100

1	2	3	4	5	6	7	8	9	10
11	12	13	14	15	16	17	18	19	20
21	22	23	24	25	26	27	28	29	30
31	32	33	34	35	36	37	38	39	40
41	42	43	44	45	46	47	48	49	50
51	52	53	54	55	56	57	58	59	60
61	62	63	64	65	66	67	68	69	70
71	72	73	74	75	76	77	78	79	80
81	82	83	84	85	86	87	88	89	90
91	92	93	94	95	96	97	98	99	100

1	2	3	4	5	6	7	8	9	10
11	12	13	14	15	16	17	18	19	20
21	22	23	24	25	26	27	28	29	30
31	32	33	34	35	36	37	38	39	40
41	42	43	44	45	46	47	48	49	50
51	52	53	54	55	56	57	58	59	60
61	62	63	64	65	66	67	68	69	70
71	72	73	74	75	76	77	78	79	80
81	82	83	84	85	86	87	88	89	90
91	92	93	94	95	96	97	98	99	100

1	2	3	4	5	6	7	8	9	10
11	12	13	14	15	16	17	18	19	20
21	22	23	24	25	26	27	28	29	30
31	32	33	34	35	36	37	38	39	40
41	42	43	44	45	46	47	48	49	50
51	52	53	54	55	56	57	58	59	60
61	62	63	64	65	66	67	68	69	70
71	72	73	74	75	76	77	78	79	80
81	82	83	84	85	86	87	88	89	90
91	92	93	94	95	96	97	98	99	100

12 Name ....

0	10	20	30	40	50
— 0	— 10	— 20	— 30	— 40	— 50
— 9	— 19	— 29	— 39	— 49
— 8	— 18	— 28	— 38	— 48
— 7	— 17	— 27	— 37	— 47
— 6	— 16	— 26	— 36	— 46
— 5	— 15	— 25	— 35	— 45
— 4	— 14	— 24	— 34	— 44
— 3	— 13	— 23	— 33	— 43
— 2	— 12	— 22	— 32	— 42
— 1	— 11	— 21	— 31	— 41
— 0	Attach here	Attach here	Attach here	Attach here

Numeracy Focus 2: Games and Activity Support Sheets

© P. Latham, H. Williams, M. Askew and S. Ebbutt 2001. Rigby
For copyright restrictions see reverse of title page.

13 Name

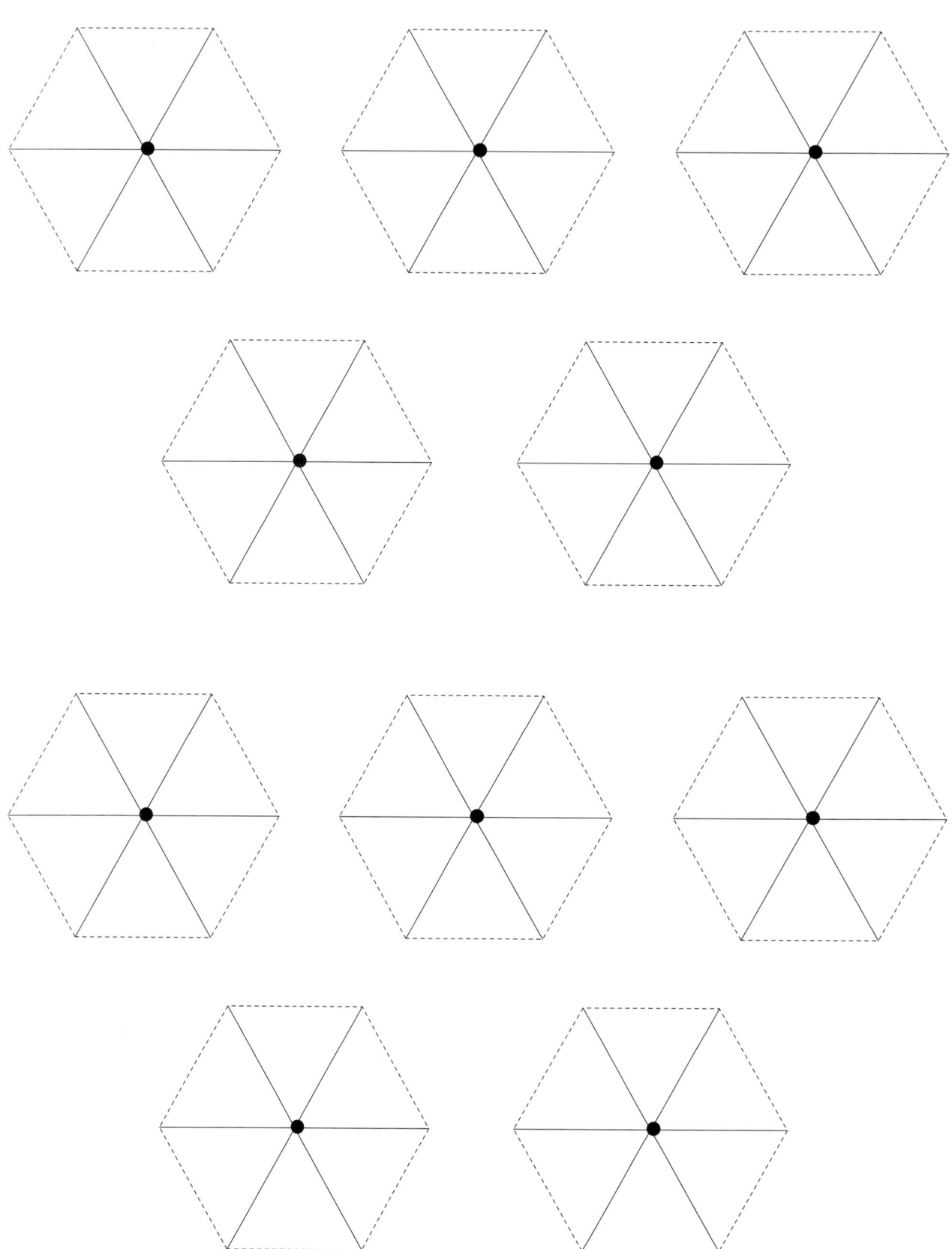

Numeracy Focus 2: Games and Activity Support Sheets

14 Name

15 Name ....

101	102	103	104	105	106	107	108	109	110
111	112	113	114	115	116	117	118	119	120
121	122	123	124	125	126	127	128	129	130
131	132	133	134	135	136	137	138	139	140
141	142	143	144	145	146	147	148	149	150
151	152	153	154	155	156	157	158	159	160
161	162	163	164	165	166	167	168	169	170
171	172	173	174	175	176	177	178	179	180
181	182	183	184	185	186	187	188	189	190
191	192	193	194	195	196	197	198	199	200

16 Name ----------

17 Name ....

0	1	2	3	4	5	6	7	8	9
10	11	12	13	14	15	16	17	18	19
20	21	22	23	24	25	26	27	28	29
30	31	32	33	34	35	36	37	38	39
40	41	42	43	44	45	46	47	48	49
50	51	52	53	54	55	56	57	58	59
60	61	62	63	64	65	66	67	68	69
70	71	72	73	74	75	76	77	78	79
80	81	82	83	84	85	86	87	88	89
90	91	92	93	94	95	96	97	98	99

18 Name

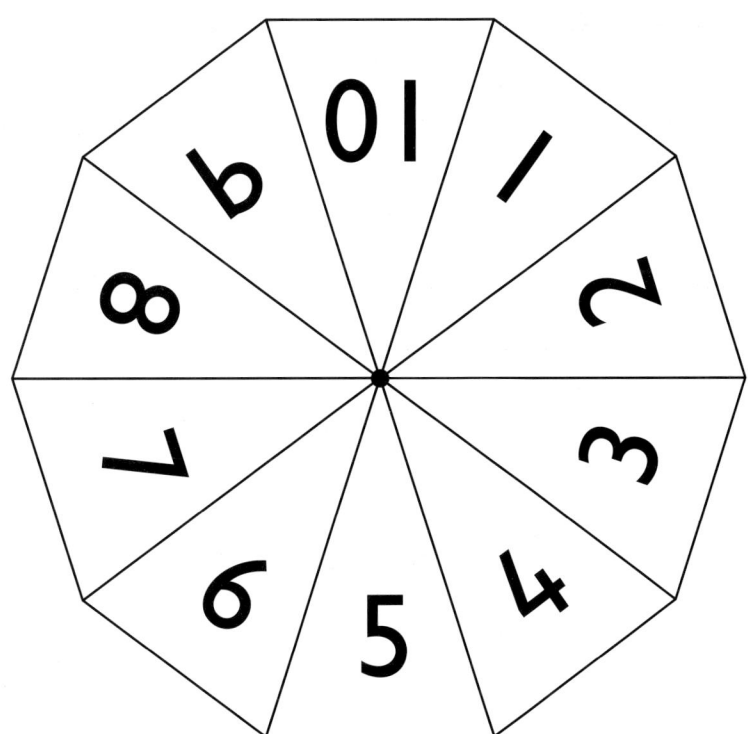

Numeracy Focus 2: Games and Activity Support Sheets

Numeracy Focus 2: Games and Activity Support Sheets

© P. Latham, H. Williams, M. Askew and S. Ebbutt 2001. Rigby
For copyright restrictions see reverse of title page.

one		eleven
two	twenty	twelve
three	thirty	thirteen
four	forty	fourteen
five	fifty	fifteen
six	sixty	sixteen
seven	seventy	seventeen
eight	eighty	eighteen
nine	ninety	nineteen

Name ....

1st	2nd	3rd
4th	5th	6th
7th	8th	9th
10th		

23 Name

11th	12th	13th
14th	15th	16th
17th	18th	19th
20th		

Numeracy Focus 2: Games and Activity Support Sheets

24 Name ....

first	second	third
fourth	fifth	sixth
seventh	eighth	ninth
tenth		

Numeracy Focus 2: Games and Activity Support Sheets

25 Name ....

eleventh	twelfth	thirteenth
fourteenth	fifteenth	sixteenth
seventeenth	eighteenth	nineteenth
twentieth		

Numeracy Focus 2: Games and Activity Support Sheets

26 Name ....

0	1	2
3	4	5
6	7	8
9	10	

Numeracy Focus 2: Games and Activity Support Sheets

© P. Latham, H. Williams, M. Askew and S. Ebbutt 2001. Rigby
For copyright restrictions see reverse of title page.

27 Name ....

15	20
14	19
13	18
12	17
11	16

Numeracy Focus 2: Games and Activity Support Sheets

28 Name ....

1	500
2	400
3	300
4	200
5	100

Numeracy Focus 2: Games and Activity Support Sheets

29 Name

6	0 0 0
7	0 0 8
8	0 0 7
9	0 0 9

Numeracy Focus 2: Games and Activity Support Sheets

30 Name ....

1 0	
2 0	0 6
3 0	0 8
4 0	0 7
5 0	0 9

Numeracy Focus 2: Games and Activity Support Sheets

© P. Latham, H. Williams, M. Askew and S. Ebbutt 2001. Rigby
For copyright restrictions see reverse of title page.

$1 \times 2 = 2$

$2 \times 2 = 4$

$3 \times 2 = 6$

$4 \times 2 = 8$

$5 \times 2 = 10$

$6 \times 2 = 12$

$7 \times 2 = 14$

$8 \times 2 = 16$

$9 \times 2 = 18$

$10 \times 2 = 20$

$1 \times 5 = 5$

$2 \times 5 = 10$

$3 \times 5 = 15$

$4 \times 5 = 20$

$5 \times 5 = 25$

$6 \times 5 = 30$

$7 \times 5 = 35$

$8 \times 5 = 40$

$9 \times 5 = 45$

$10 \times 5 = 50$

$1 \times 10 = 10$

$2 \times 10 = 20$

$3 \times 10 = 30$

$4 \times 10 = 40$

$5 \times 10 = 50$

$6 \times 10 = 60$

$7 \times 10 = 70$

$8 \times 10 = 80$

$9 \times 10 = 90$

$10 \times 10 = 100$

34 Name --

35 Name ----------

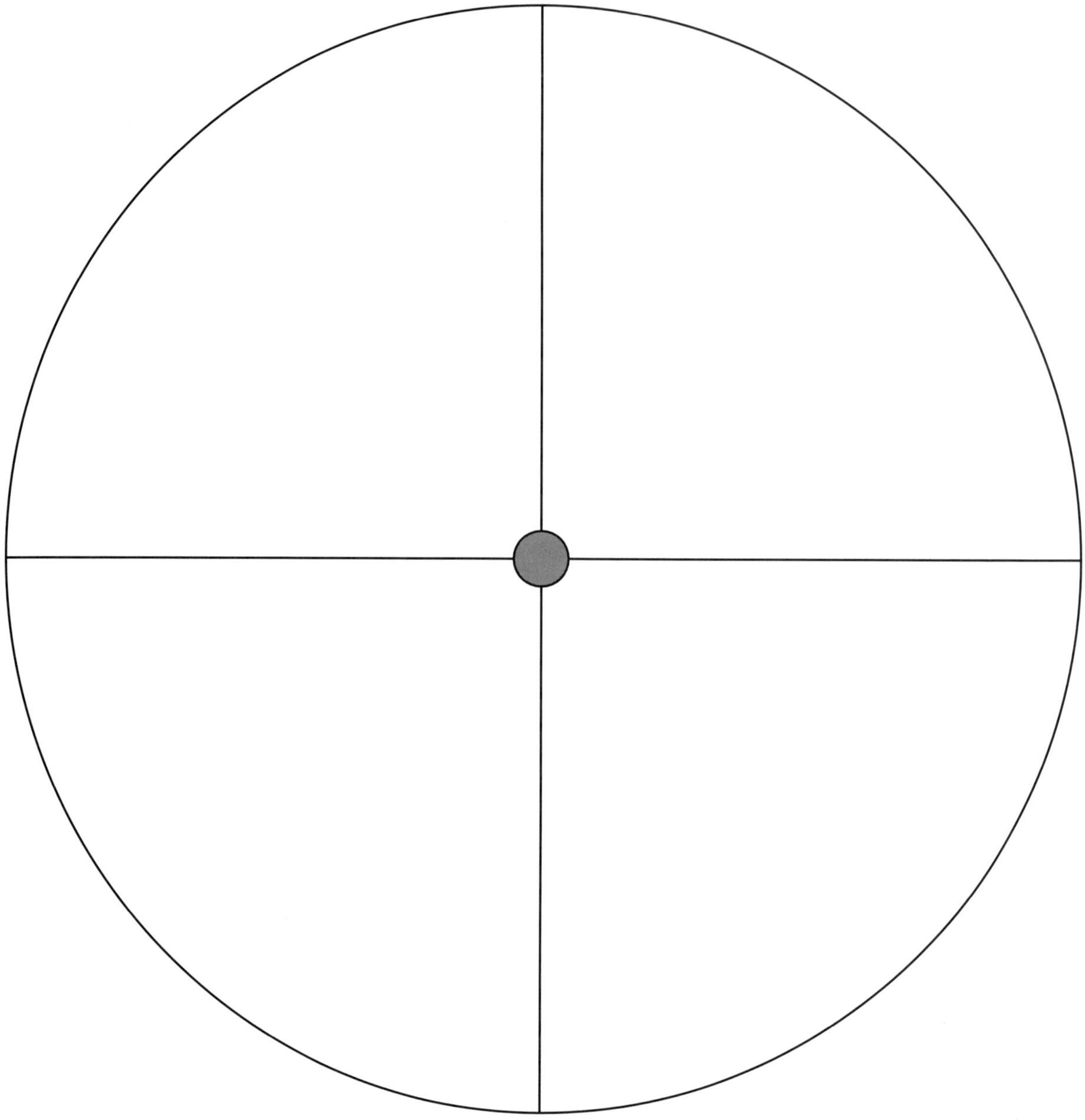

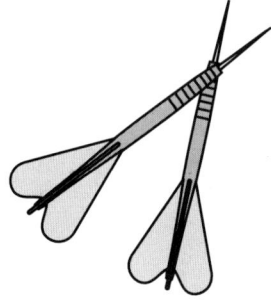

Numeracy Focus 2: Games and Activity Support Sheets

36 Name ....

Numeracy Focus 2: Games and Activity Support Sheets

37 Name ....

The highest jump ever recorded measured 2 metres and 45 centimetres

The longest jump ever recorded measured 8 metres and 95 centimetres

The shortest person ever measured 57 centimetres

The tallest person ever measured 2 metres and 72 centimetres

38 Name ....

Roll the two dice together.
If the total dice score is odd, stay where you are.
If the total dice score is even, move your counter one space.
The first to reach the top is the winner.

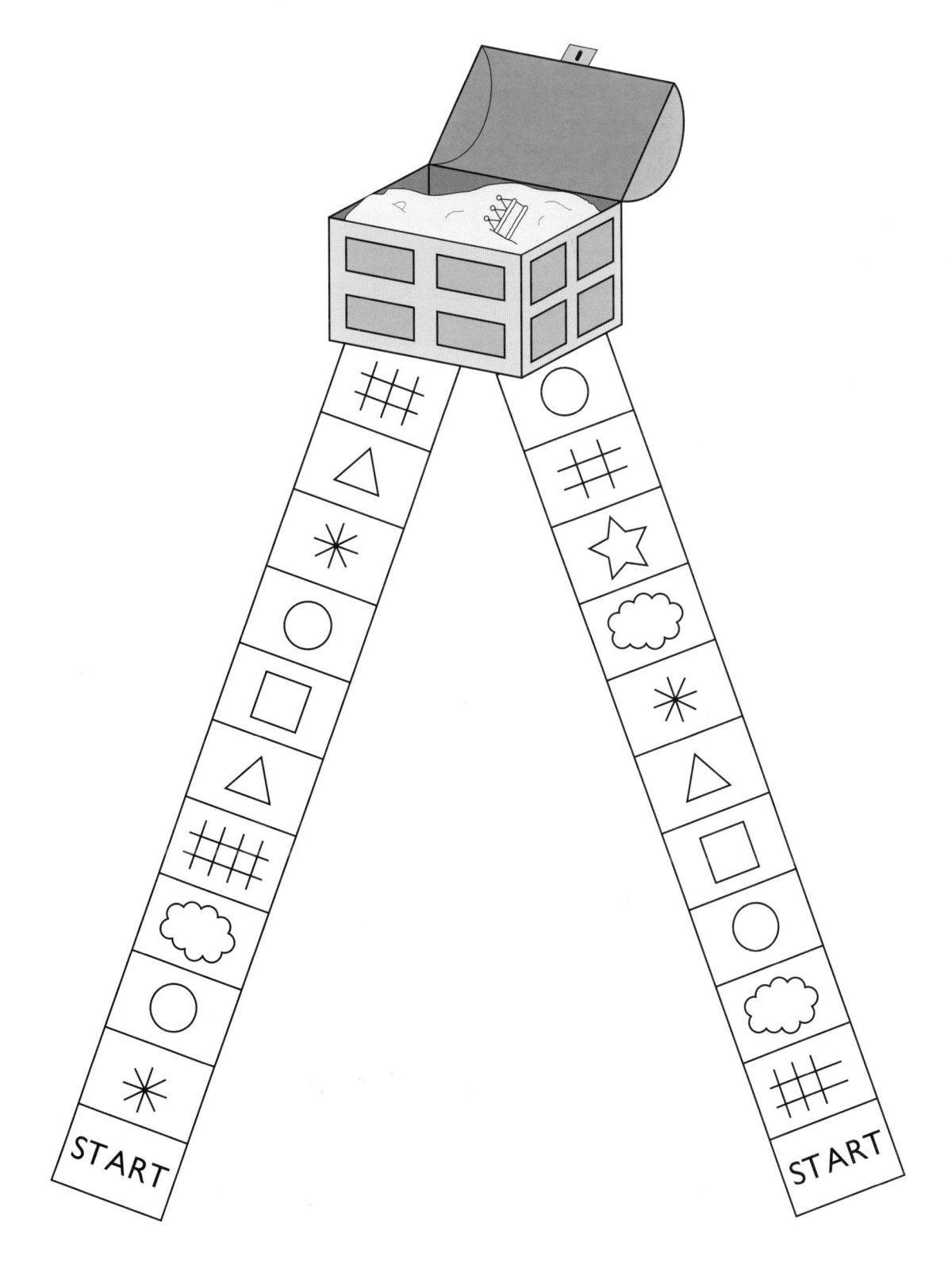

39 Name ----------

Numeracy Focus 2: Games and Activity Support Sheets

Mrs Smith's Shopping List

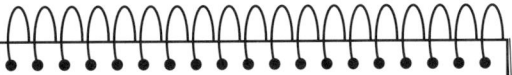

1 kg Bananas
6 kg Potatoes
5 kg Turkey drumsticks
1 kg Sausages
3 kg Dog biscuits
4 kg Box washing powder

Mrs Smith brings her shopping home in two boxes.
How does she pack the boxes so that she has:
- The same mass in each box?
- One box 2 kilograms heavier than the other?

41

Leon's parcel was about one kilogram heavy.

Ann's parcel had a mass of one-and-a-quarter kilograms.

Claire's parcel weighed half a kilogram.

David's parcel was the lightest.

Tyson's parcel was the second heaviest.

Guzzler the Greedy Giant's Shopping List

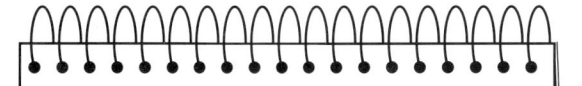

- 5 kg Bananas
- 12 kg Potatoes
- 10 kg Turkey drumsticks
- 6 kg Sausages
- 9 kg Dog biscuits

43 Name ....

Numeracy Focus 2: Games and Activity Support Sheets

© P. Latham, H. Williams, M. Askew and S. Ebbutt 2001. Rigby
For copyright restrictions see reverse of title page.

44 Name ....

Numeracy Focus 2: Games and Activity Support Sheets

© P. Latham, H. Williams, M. Askew and S. Ebbutt 2001. Rigby
For copyright restrictions see reverse of title page.

Money trail

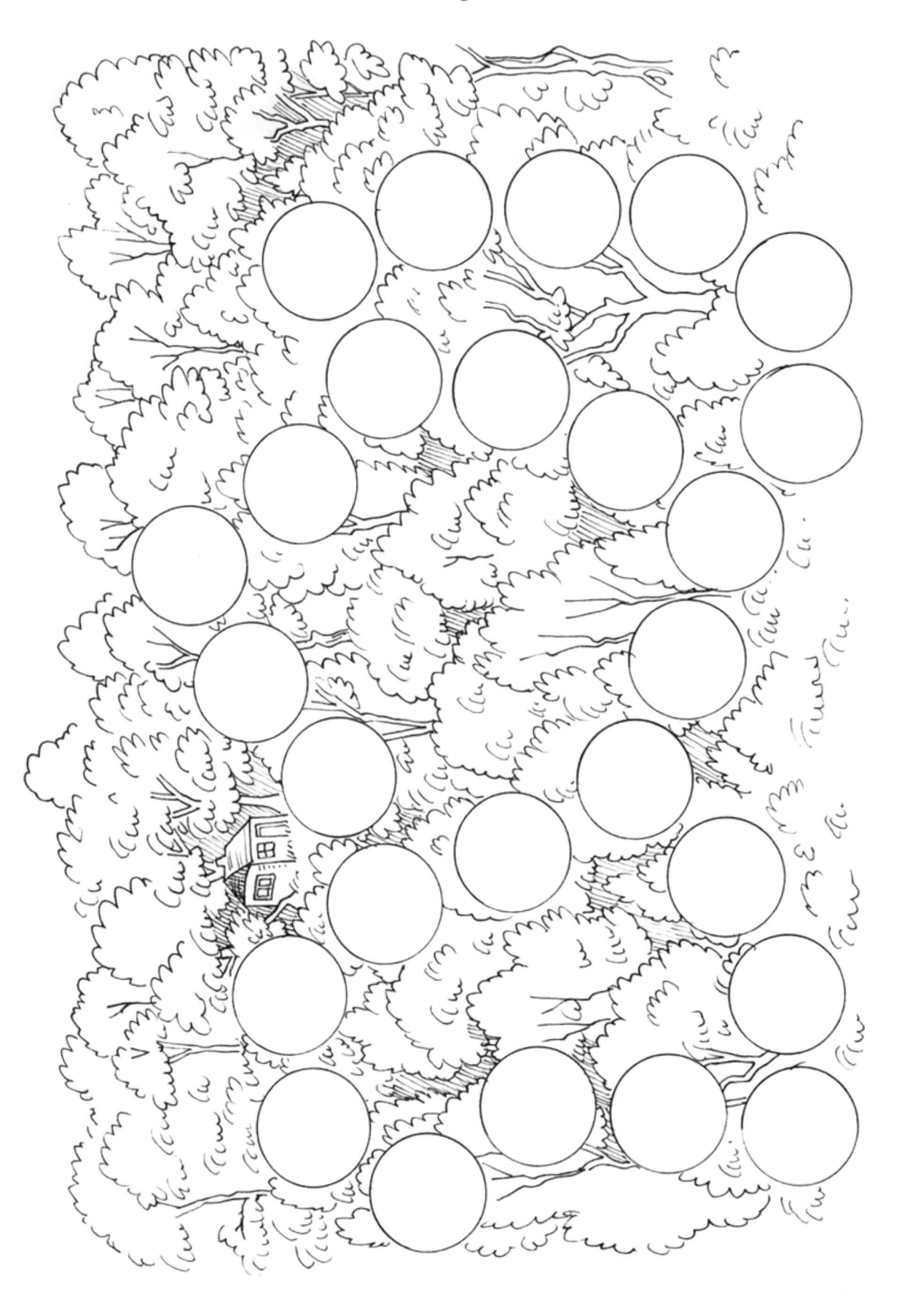

46 Name

Who will reach the tower?

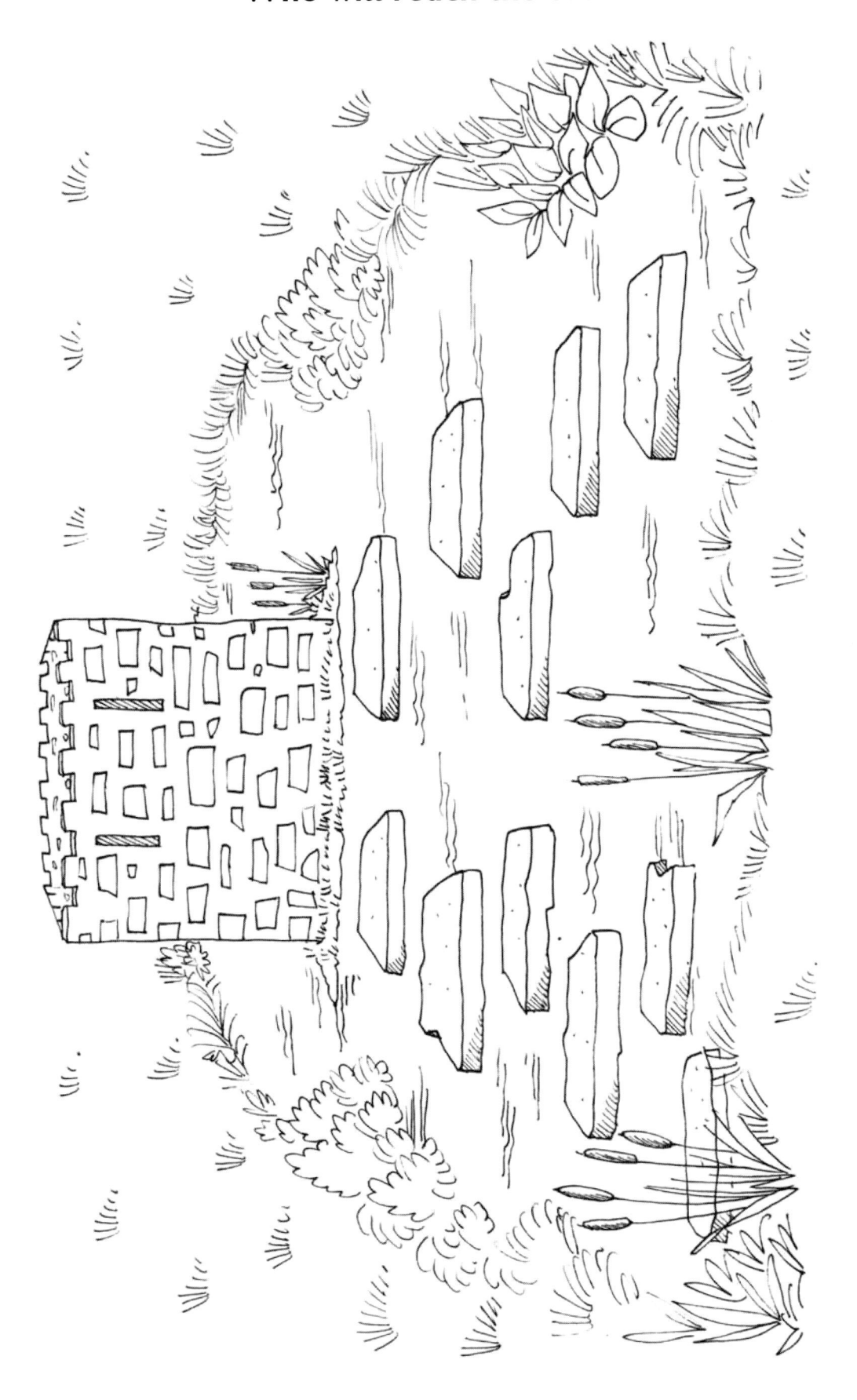

Numeracy Focus 2: Games and Activity Support Sheets

47 Name ....

START

					35			1
								2
								3

55

25   FINISH

45

15

Numeracy Focus 2: Games and Activity Support Sheets

48 Name ....

1	2	3		5
6			9	
		13		
16				
			24	

For the teacher

1. Children play in pairs. Each player needs a counter or a cube.
2. The players take turns to place their cube on a blank square.
3. Then they ask their partner to say what that number should be.
4. They write the numbers in the squares.
5. When the grid is complete, children take turns to place a cube on a square and ask their partner to say what number it covers.

Numeracy Focus 2: Games and Activity Support Sheets

© P. Latham, H. Williams, M. Askew and S. Ebbutt 2001. Rigby
For copyright restrictions see reverse of title page.

1	2	3	4	5	6	7	8	9	10
11	12	13	14	15	16	17	18	19	20
21	22		24	25	26		28		30
31	32		34	35	36		38		40
41	42		44	45	46		48		50
51	52						58		60
61	62		64	65	66		68		70
71	72		74	75	76		78		80
81	82		84	85	86		88		90
91	92	93	94	95	96	97	98	99	100

50

0	10	8	2
8	2	3	5
7	3	7	5
2	1	6	4
1	9	8	5
0	8	9	2

Numeracy Focus 2: Games and Activity Support Sheets

51

add 2 = | + 2 =

Numeracy Focus 2: Games and Activity Support Sheets

© P. Latham, H. Williams, M. Askew and S. Ebbutt 2001. Rigby
For copyright restrictions see reverse of title page.

52 Names

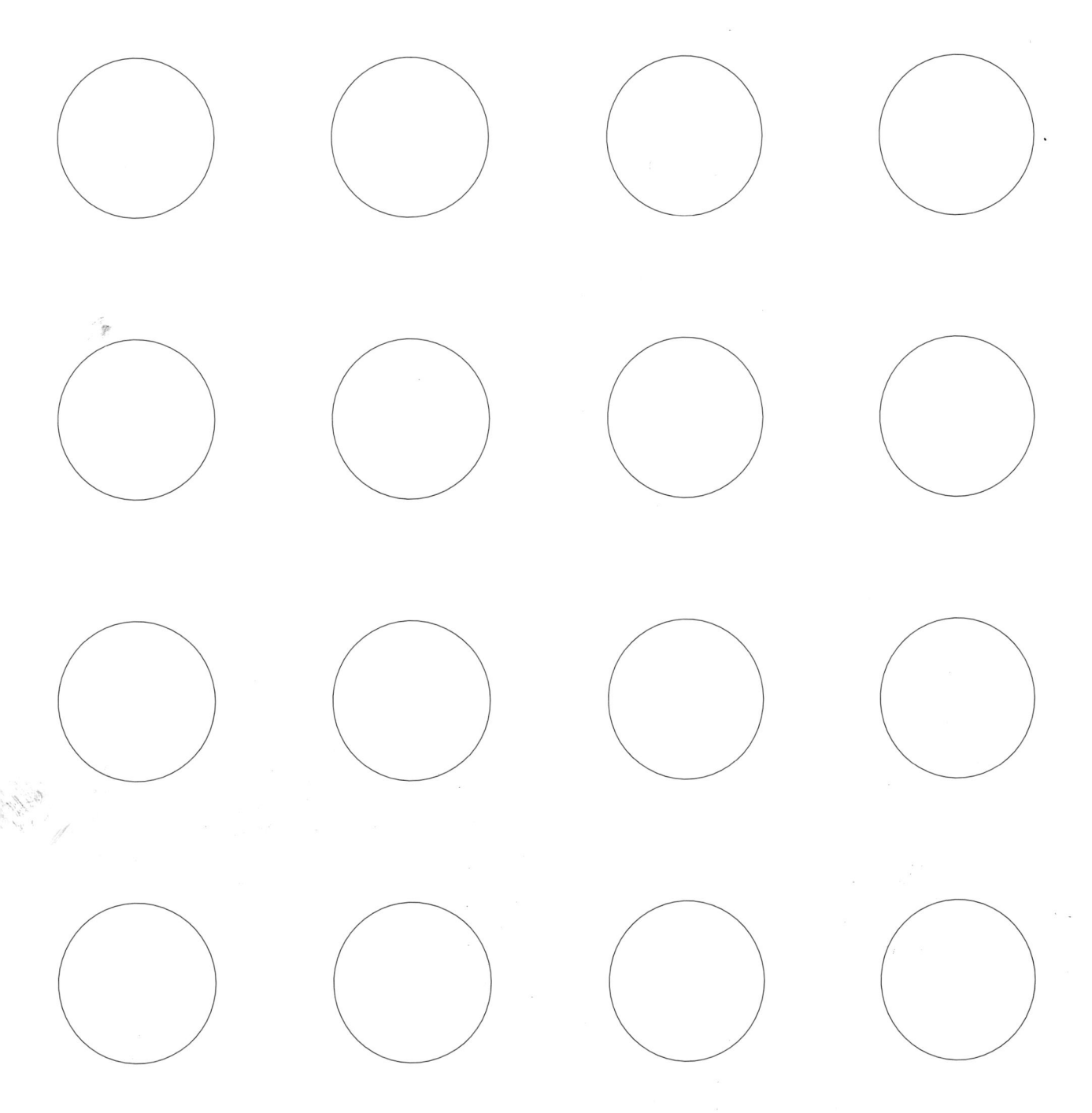

53 Name _____

Numeracy Focus 2: Games and Activity Support Sheets

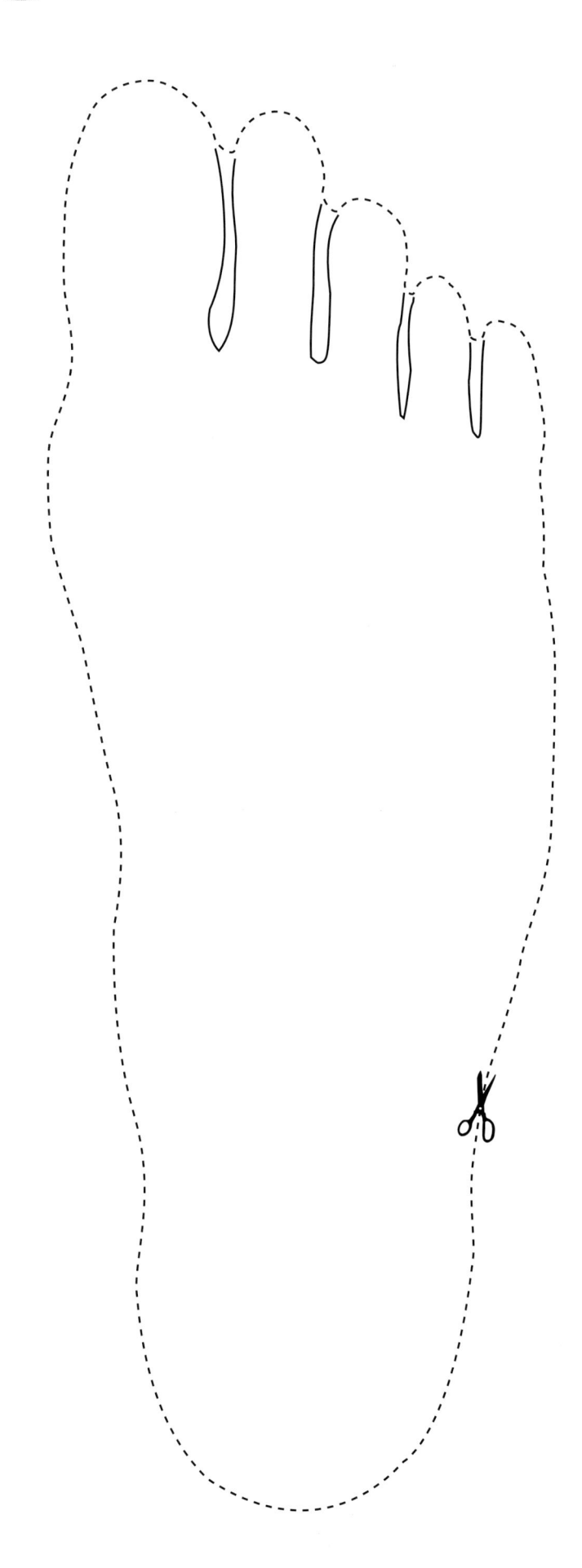

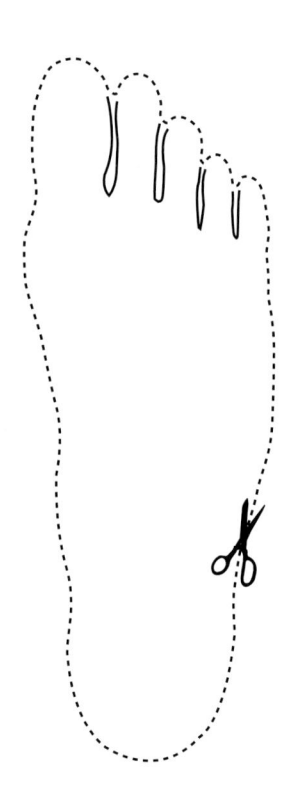

© P. Latham, H. Williams, M. Askew and S. Ebbutt 2001. Rigby
For copyright restrictions see reverse of title page.

Elastic band	Start length	Stretched length	It grew by...
1			
2			
3			
4			
5			

55 Name --

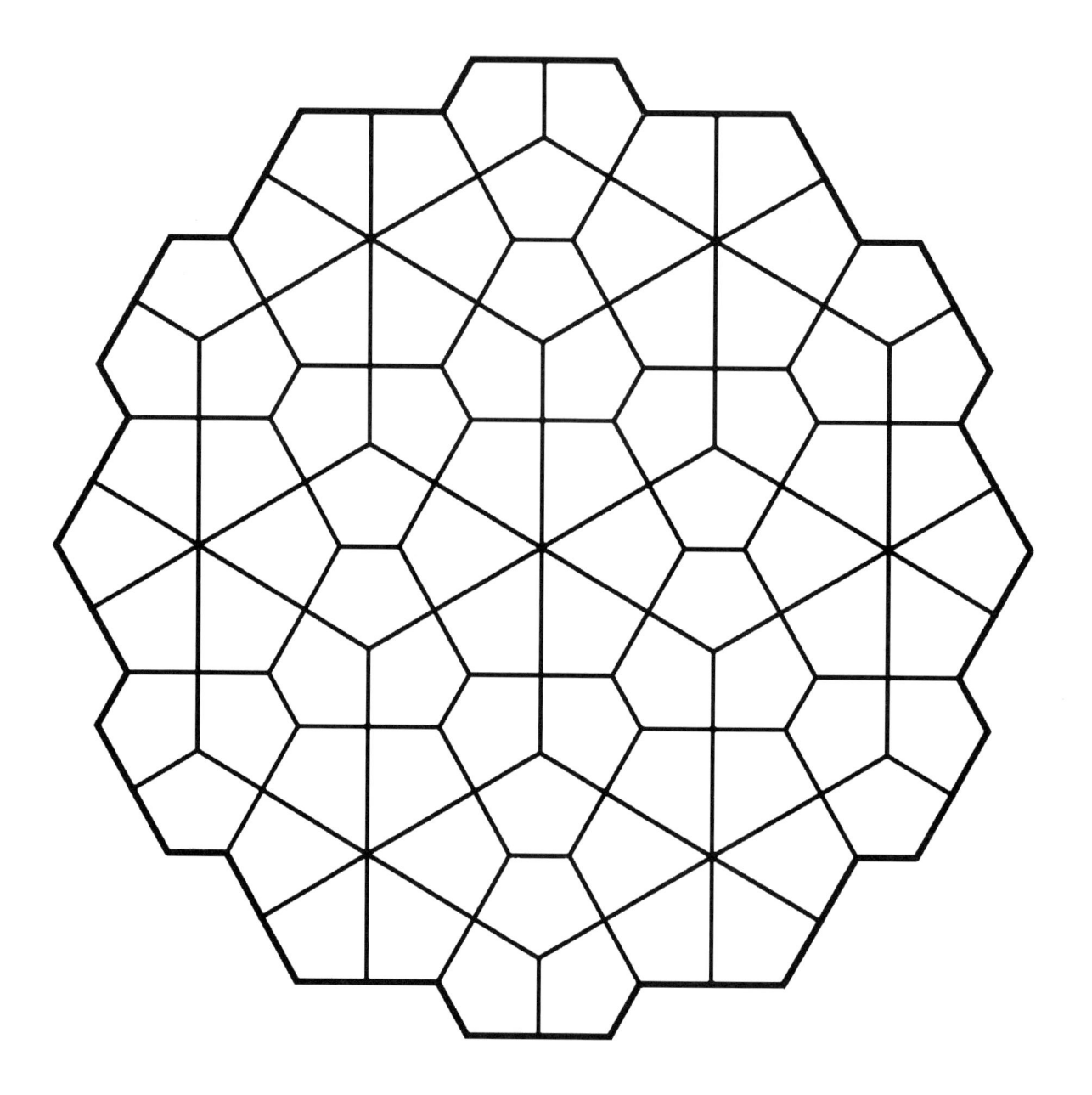

Numeracy Focus 2: Games and Activity Support Sheets

© P. Latham, H. Williams, M. Askew and S. Ebbutt 2001. Rigby
For copyright restrictions see reverse of title page.

56 Name ....

			66			

| 53 | | | 56 | 57 | | |

| | | | 36 | | | |

57 Name ....

Start at 1. Count on in 2s.
Colour the number squares you land on.

1	2	3	4
5	6	7	8
9	10	11	12
13	14	15	16

1	2	3	4	5
6	7	8	9	10
11	12	13	14	15
16	17	18	19	20
21	22	23	24	25

Describe the patterns you make: _____

_____

Numeracy Focus 2: Games and Activity Support Sheets

© P. Latham, H. Williams, M. Askew and S. Ebbutt 2001. Rigby
For copyright restrictions see reverse of title page.

58 Name

Complete the number star from the centre.
Follow the rules of the arrows.

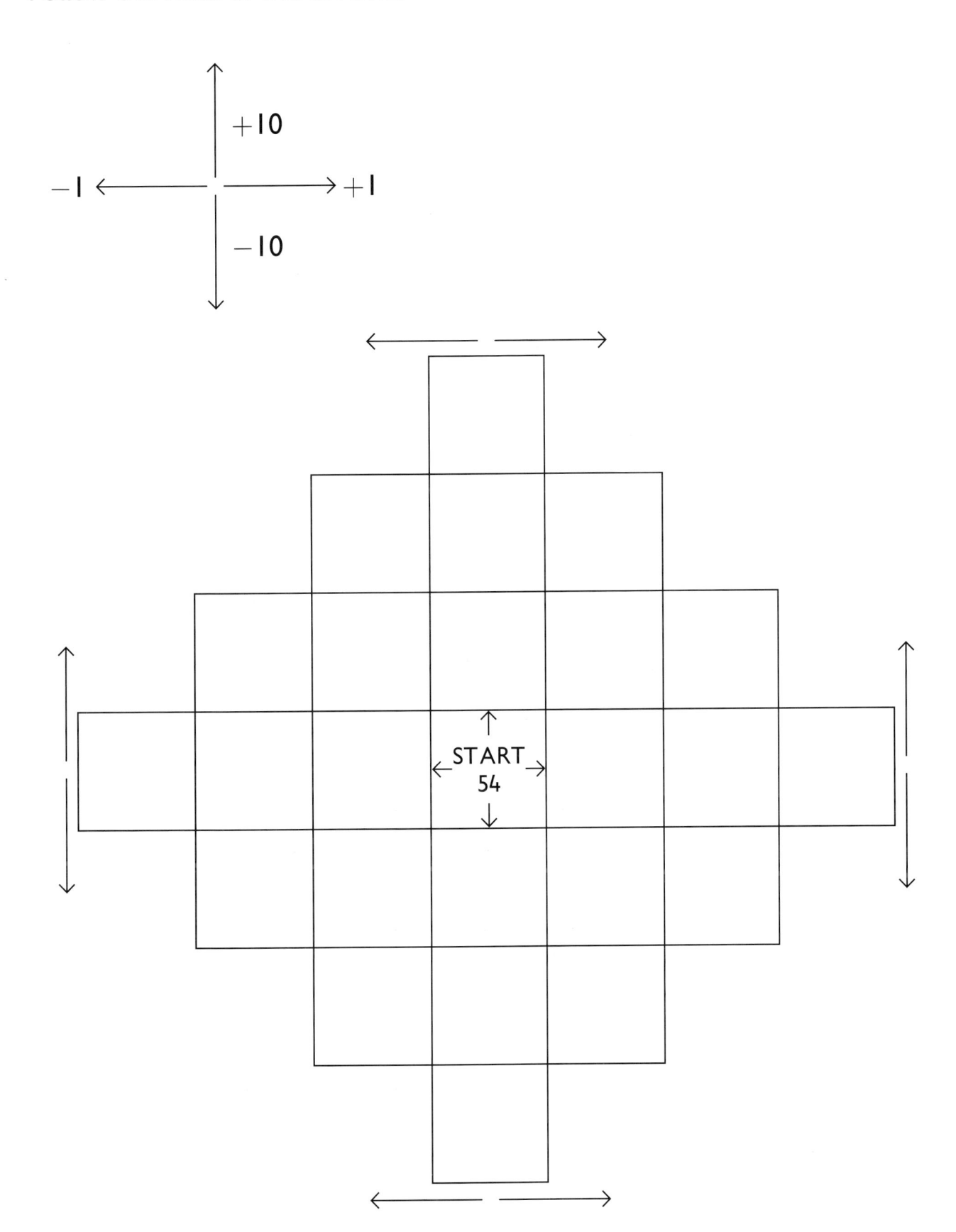

+10
−1   +1
−10

START
54

Numeracy Focus 2: Games and Activity Support Sheets

59 Name --

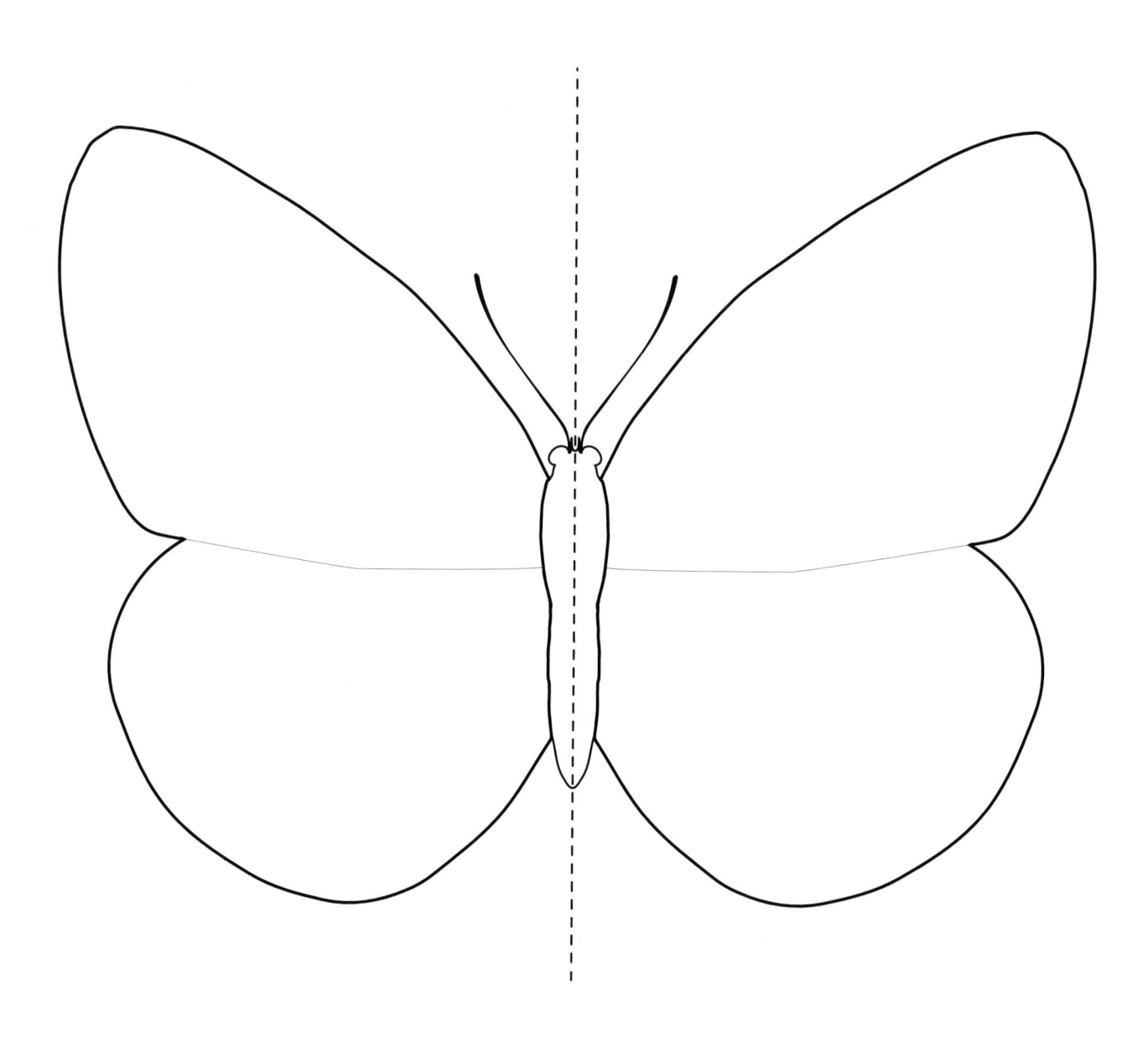

Numeracy Focus 2: Games and Activity Support Sheets

60 Name ....

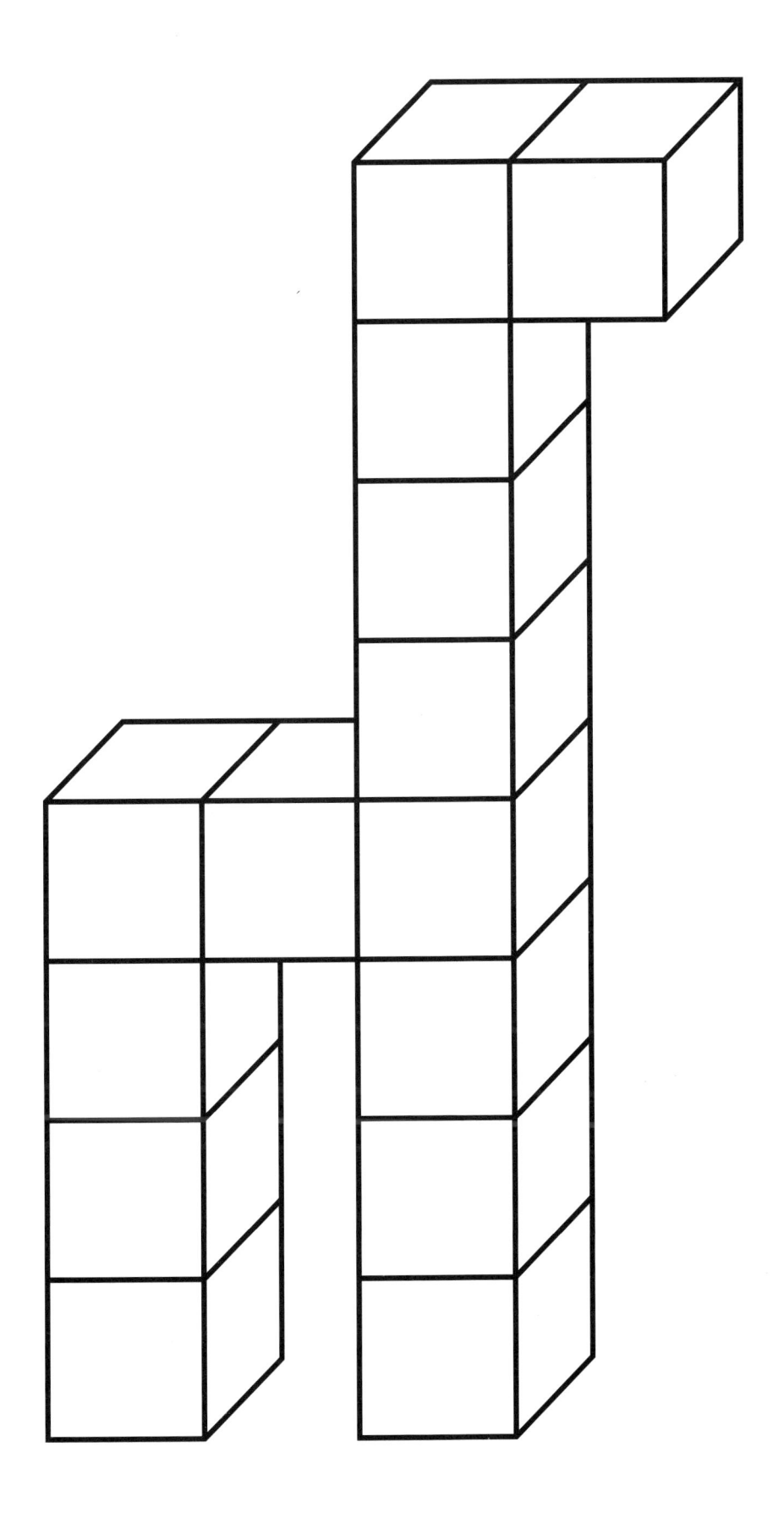

Numeracy Focus 2: Games and Activity Support Sheets

61 Name ....

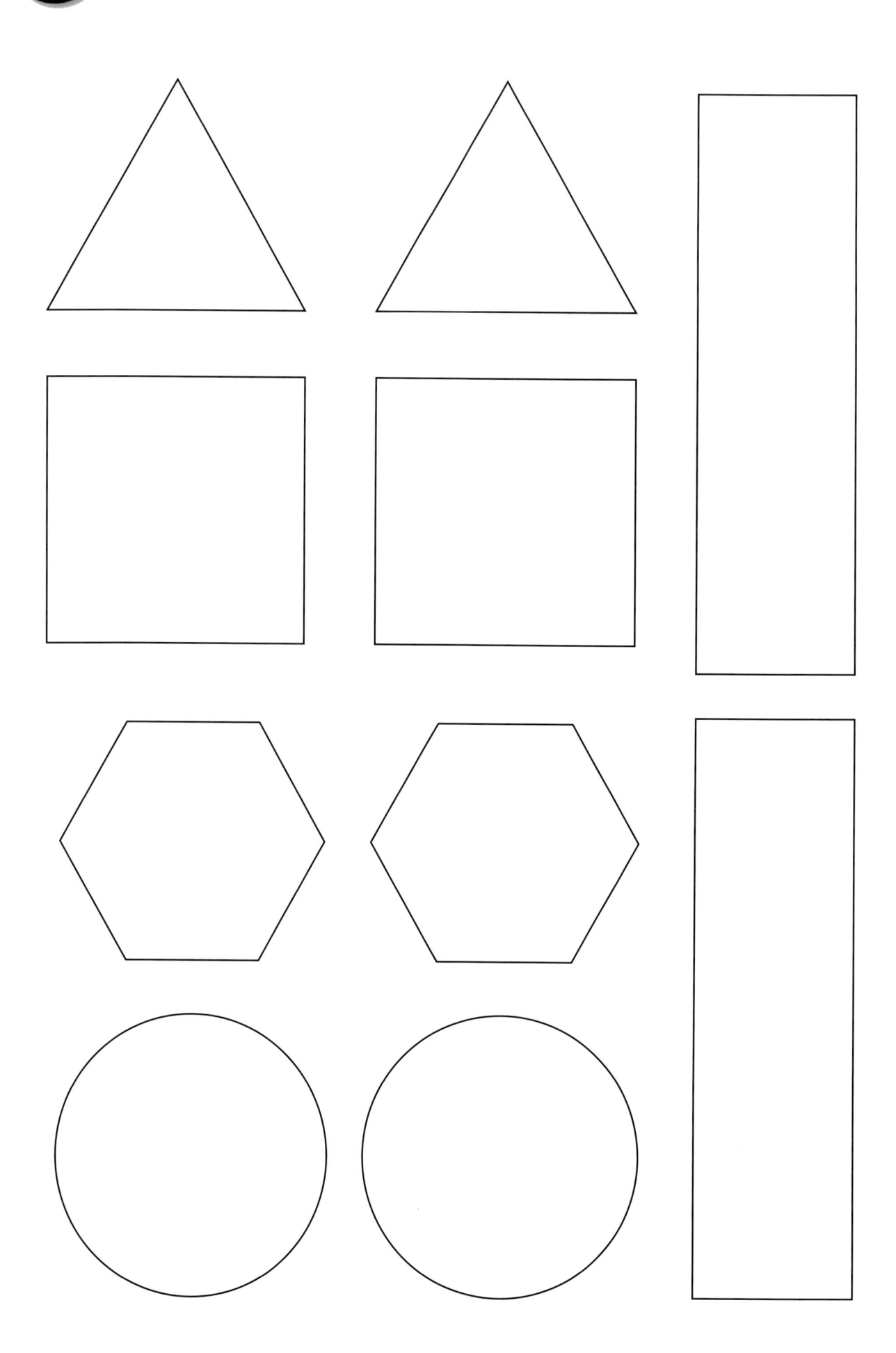

Numeracy Focus 2: Games and Activity Support Sheets

© P. Latham, H. Williams, M. Askew and S. Ebbutt 2001. Rigby
For copyright restrictions see reverse of title page.

Wholemeal scones

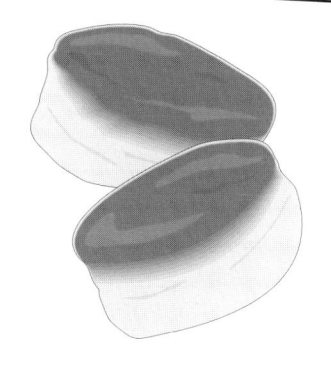

Ingredients:	Utensils:
50 g wholemeal flour	mixing bowl
50 g self raising flour	spoons
25 g margarine	balance scales
25 g grated cheese	50 g weight
milk to mix	rolling pin
	pastry cutter
	baking tray

1. Weigh both the flours. Weigh the margarine.
2. Rub the margarine and the flours together until it looks like breadcrumbs.
3. Weigh and add the cheese and stir the mixture.
4. Add a little milk and mix to form a dough.
5. Roll out on a floured board until the dough is about two-and-a-half centimetres thick.
6. Cut into rounds and place on the baking tray.
7. Bake for approximately 10–15 minutes.

63 Name

July
February
October
September
May
December
January
August
April
March
November
June

Numeracy Focus 2: Games and Activity Support Sheets

© P. Latham, H. Williams, M. Askew and S. Ebbutt 2001. Rigby
For copyright restrictions see reverse of title page.

Name ....

Complete these tables.

Names of months beginning with 'J'	Names of months not beginning with 'J'

Names of months with 3 letters	Names of months with 4 letters	Names of months with 5 letters	Names of months with 6 letters

The first 4 months of the year	The second 4 months of the year	The third 4 months of the year

Numeracy Focus 2: Games and Activity Support Sheets

65 Name --

apples	oranges	kiwi fruit	bananas	strawberries

numbers with 2 tens	numbers with 5 tens	numbers with 0 tens	numbers with 3 tens	numbers with 7 tens

67

Name ....

My favourite number is ....

favourite numbers which are greater than mine	favourite numbers which are less than mine

Numeracy Focus 2: Games and Activity Support Sheets

68 Name

			Number of counters

Numeracy Focus 2: Games and Activity Support Sheets

69 Name

For the teacher

1. In pairs, the children shuffle the number cards and place them face down in a pile.
2. Ask the children to label the boxes on the sides of the diagram such as, 'odd numbers', 'even numbers', 'numbers under 20' and 'numbers over 20'.
3. The children take turns to take a card from the pile and place it in the correct part of the diagram, according to the labels.
4. When all the cards have been placed, ask the children how many cards are in each section and which one has the most cards.

14	34
78	15
93	52
27	60
82	19
46	66
71	11
98	74
55	12
43	21

12	48
15	27
43	17
33	32
44	25
11	21
36	18
41	23
14	22
40	19

72 Names ....

9	2	5	8	3	6
4	6	8	1	7	3
2	6	7	8	2	4

Front / Back

Numeracy Focus 2: Games and Activity Support Sheets

73 Name

Numbers	cards	words
26		
34		
21		
14		

1	2	2	3	3	4	4	5
5	6	6	7	7	8	8	9
9	10	10	11	11	12	12	13
13	14	14	15				

Numeracy Focus 2: Games and Activity Support Sheets

75 Names

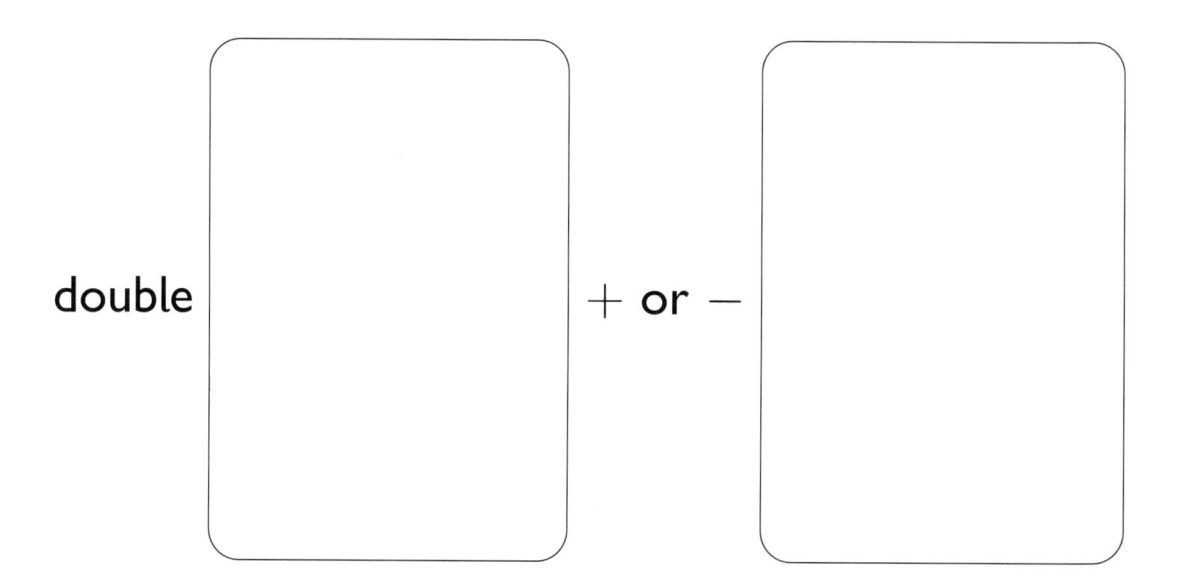

double [ ] + or − [ ]

Numeracy Focus 2: Games and Activity Support Sheets

76 Name ....

Numbers in oval: 4, 15, 12, 6, 9, 5, 1, 13, 2, 11, 10, 7, 8, 14, 3

36	12	30	38
2	7	16	24
14	35	0	28
6	18	32	20

Numeracy Focus 2: Games and Activity Support Sheets

I spent 20p	I spent 10p	I spent 30p
I spent 50p	I spent 40p	I spent 25p
I spent 60p	I spent 80p	I spent 70p
I spent 90p	I spent 99p	I spent 100p
I spent 75p	I spent 95p	I spent 2p
My change is 80p	My change is 90p	My change is 70p
My change is 50p	My change is 60p	My change is 75p
My change is 40p	My change is 20p	My change is 30p
My change is 10p	My change is 1p	My change is 0p
My change is 25p	My change is 5p	My change is 98p

78 Name

Object	Estimate	Mass
	about 3 kg	just over 2 kg

79 Name

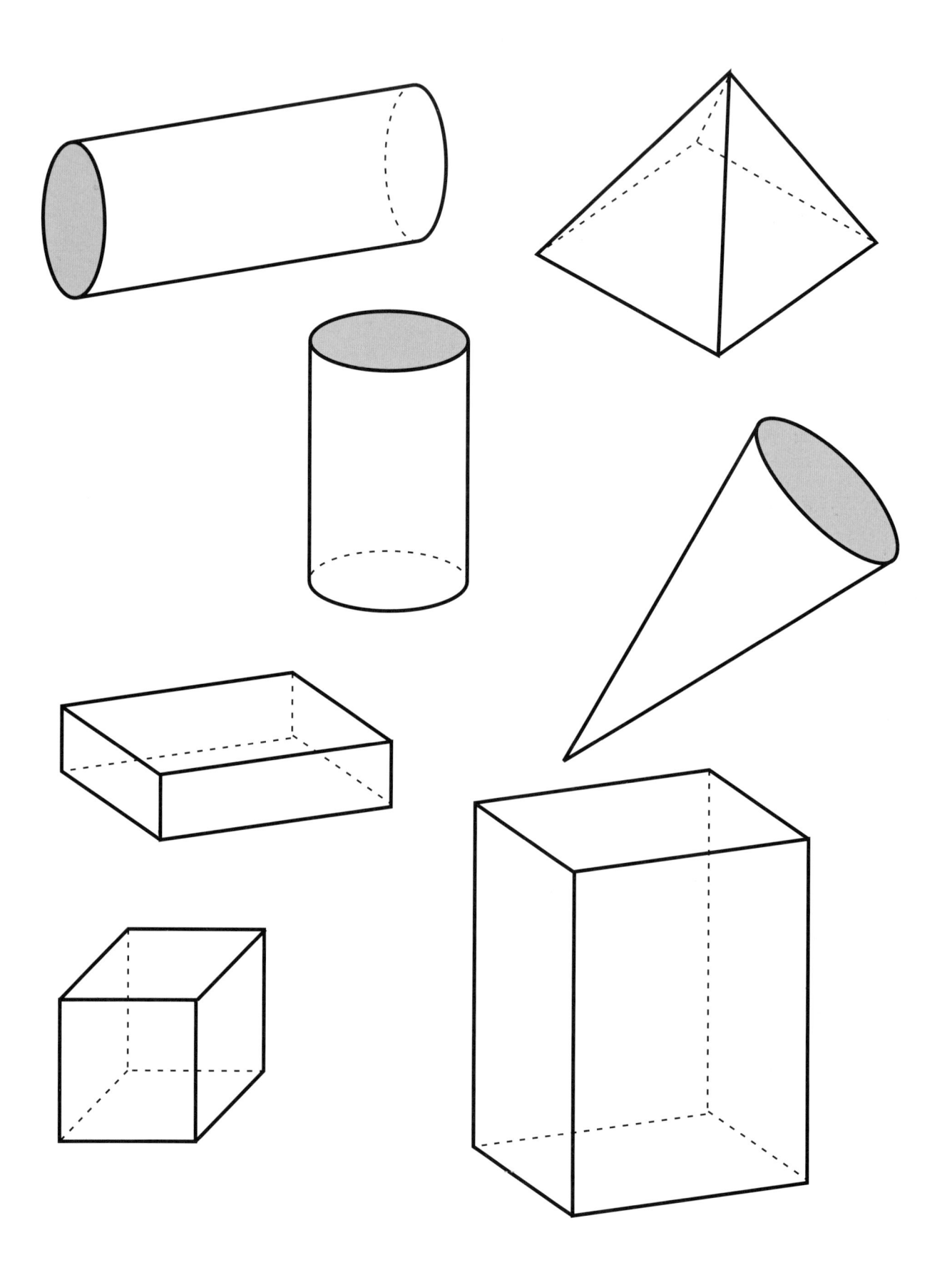

80 Name ....

My first box is a _____

How many faces? ☐

How many edges? ☐

How many corners? ☐

My second box is a _____

How many faces? ☐

How many edges? ☐

How many corners? ☐

My third box is a _____

How many faces? ☐

How many edges? ☐

How many corners? ☐

My fourth box is a _____

How many faces? ☐

How many edges? ☐

How many corners? ☐

81 Name

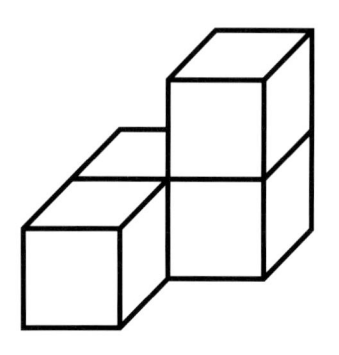

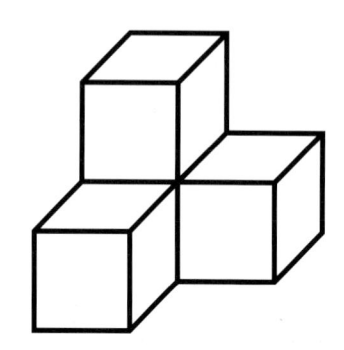

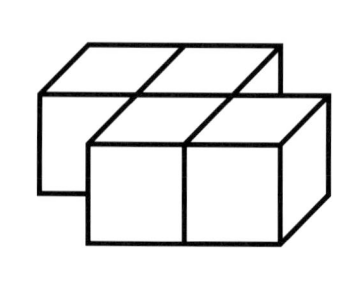

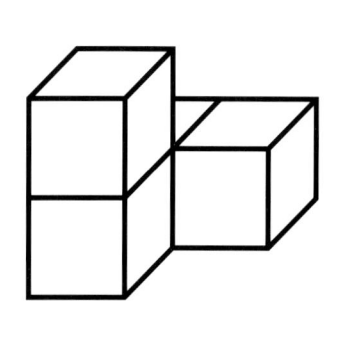

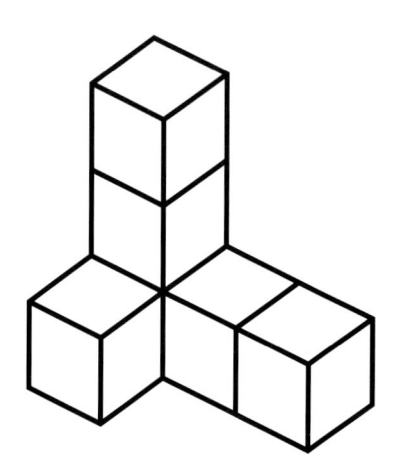

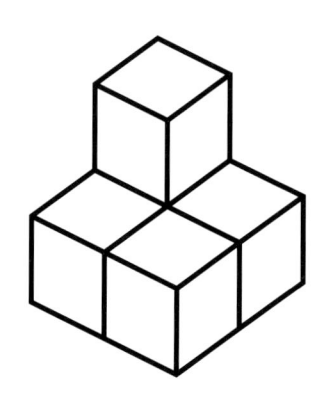

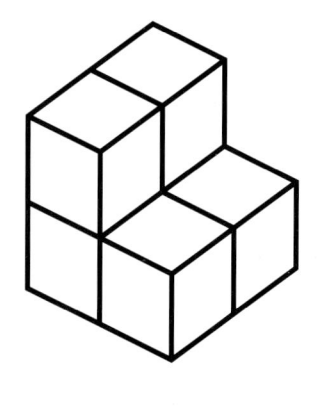

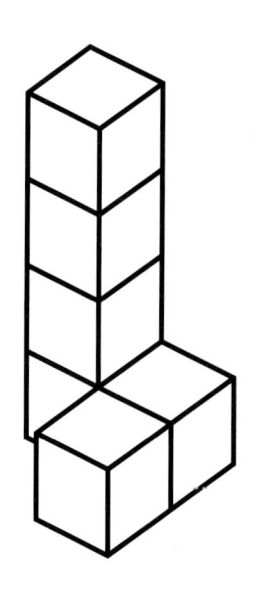

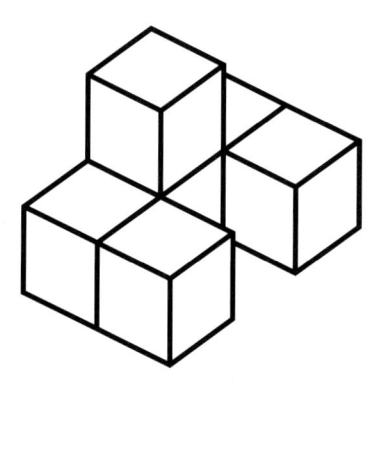

82 Name

For the teacher

1. Before you give a copy of the sheet to each child, write a different number, either 2, 3, 4 or 5, in each 'COUNT ON' box.
2. The children write a number less than ten in the first 'input' tube then work out and write the answer in the 'output' tube, based on the 'count on' number for that machine.
3. They do the same for each machine, with a different number each time in the 'input' tubes.

Numeracy Focus 2: Games and Activity Support Sheets

© P. Latham, H. Williams, M. Askew and S. Ebbutt 2001. Rigby
For copyright restrictions see reverse of title page.

83 Name

十	二十	三十	四十	五十		
九	十九	二十九	三十九	四十九		
八	十八	二十八	三十八	四十八		
七	十七	二十七	三十七	四十七		
六	十六	二十六	三十六	四十六		
五	十五	二十五	三十五	四十五		
四	十四	二十四	三十四	四十四		
三	十三	二十三	三十三	四十三		
二	十二	二十二	三十二	四十二		
一	十	二十	三十	四十		

Numeracy Focus 2: Games and Activity Support Sheets

85 Name

My equal numbers book

Numeracy Focus 2: Games and Activity Support Sheets

86 Name ....

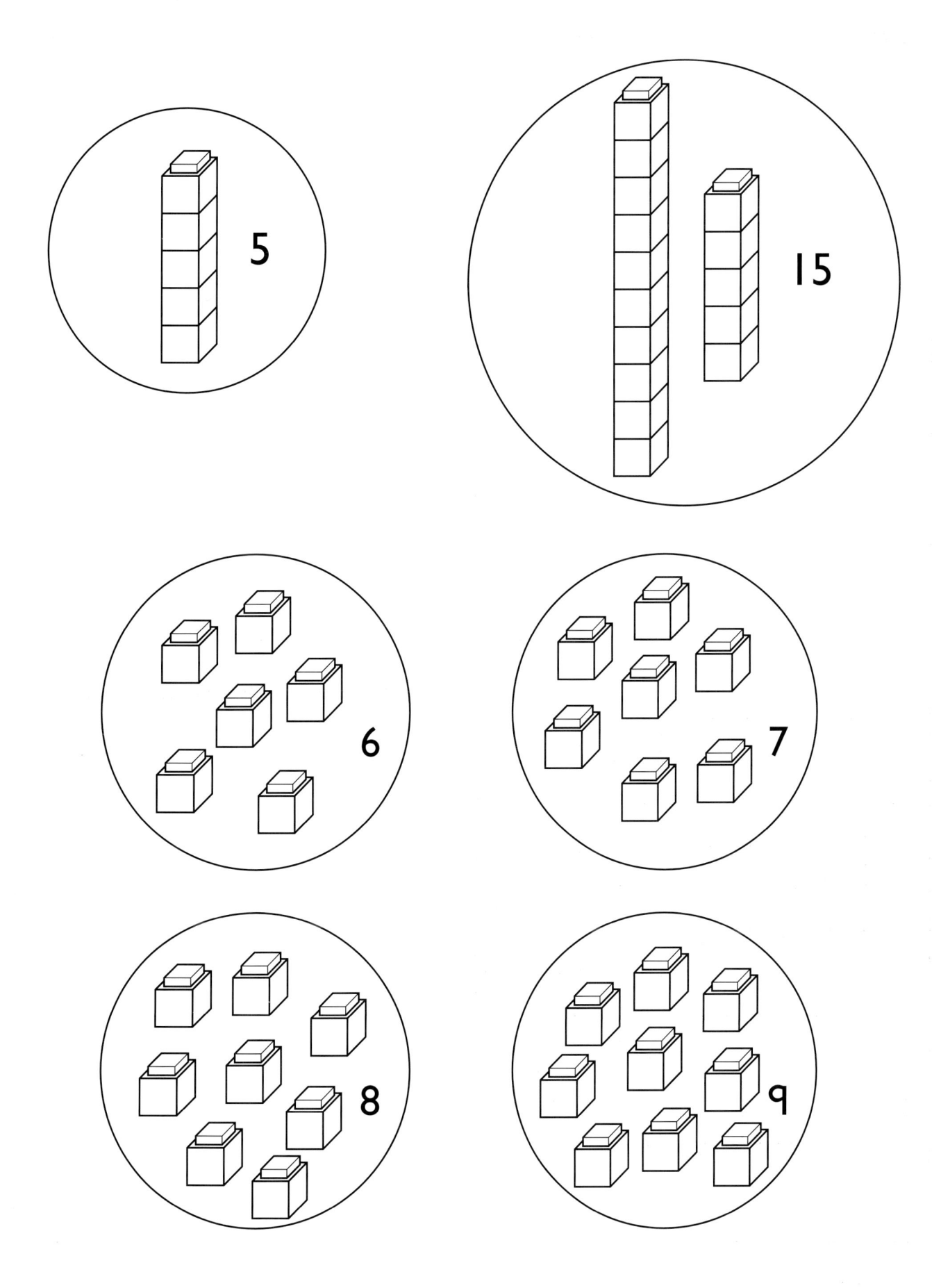

5

15

6

7

8

9

Numeracy Focus 2: Games and Activity Support Sheets

87 Name ----------

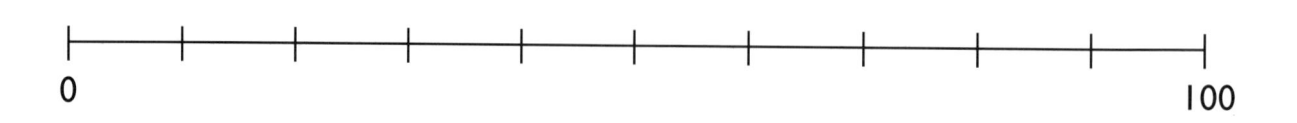

```
 |--+--+--+--+--+--+--+--+--+--|
 0                            100
```

____ + ____ = 100   ____ + ____ = 100

____ + ____ = 100   ____ + ____ = 100

____ + ____ = 100   ____ + ____ = 100

____ + ____ + ____ = 100

____ + ____ + ____ = 100

____ + ____ + ____ = 100

Numeracy Focus 2: Games and Activity Support Sheets

© P. Latham, H. Williams, M. Askew and S. Ebbutt 2001. Rigby
For copyright restrictions see reverse of title page.

88 Name

Numeracy Focus 2: Games and Activity Support Sheets

89 Name --

50	20	15	35	40	20
10	45	50	15	25	10
30	25	45	40	35	20
45	40	30	10	50	25
35	45	10	35	15	40
30	15	50	20	30	25

Numeracy Focus 2: Games and Activity Support Sheets

90 Names ....

Player 1 ....

	25		60	
5		30		20

	15		10		100	
80		60		40		20
10		15		80		25
	5		20		40	

	30		15		10	
		5		25		

Player 2 ....

Numeracy Focus 2: Games and Activity Support Sheets

91 Name ----------

Activity	How many times?	
	Estimate	Actual result
Counting interlocking cubes		

BBC2 7:00 Robot Zone	ITV 5:00 Minor celebrity!
BBC1 4:00 The Animal Show	ITV 4:00 Digipoke
ITV 7:00 Sunnydale	BBC1 5:00 Cartoonarama
BBC1 6:00 News and Weather	BBC2 4:00 Ready, Steady, Chat
ITV 6:00 Wheel of Misfortune	BBC2 5:00 Crazy Knitwear
BBC1 7:00 Puppets on Strings	BBC2 6:00 The Chimpsons

Numeracy Focus 2: Games and Activity Support Sheets

once per day	once per year	once per week
once every minute	once every hour	once per term

Numeracy Focus 2: Games and Activity Support Sheets

January	February
March	April
May	June
July	August
September	October
November	December

95 Names

Bill Twitcher's Bird-watch Diary

At 11 o'clock I saw a thrush. Then I saw three sparrows. I thought I saw a blackbird then, but it was a magpie. Six seagulls flew past me at quarter-past eleven. Then I saw four sparrows and two starlings. At half past eleven I saw another thrush. Then I saw three magpies flying together. After that I saw four more seagulls, and two more starlings. Then I saw lots of sparrows. I counted them and there were four. Just before 12 o'clock I saw two magpies and one starling.

97 Name

True or false

Favourite drinks of pupils in class 2

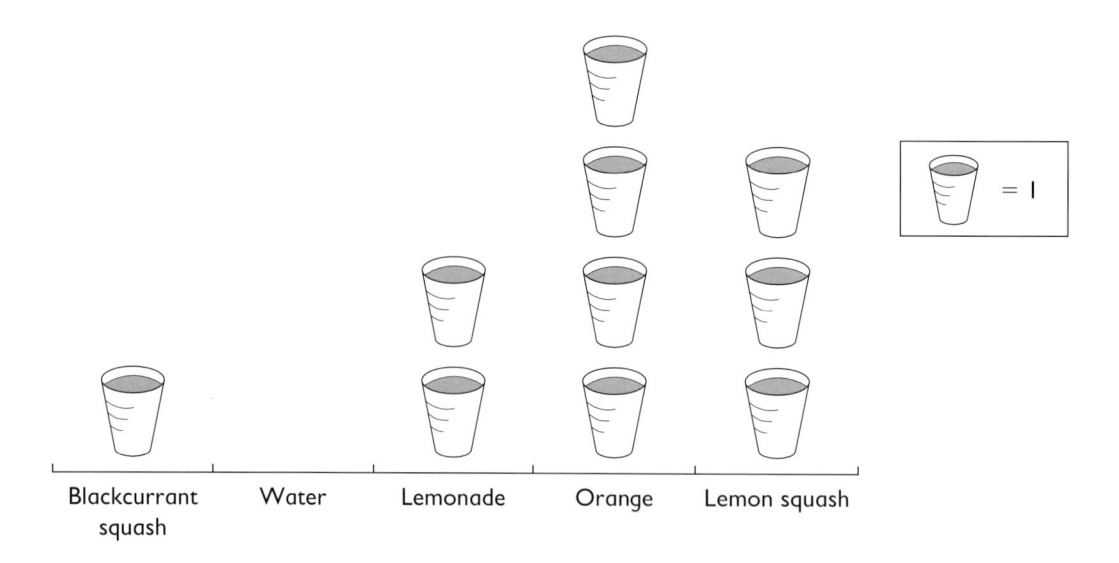

[Pictogram: Blackcurrant squash = 1, Water = 0, Lemonade = 2, Orange = 4, Lemon squash = 3. Key: 1 cup = 1]

The most popular drink is orange.

No children had water.

The least popular drink was Blackcurrant squash.

More children had lemon squash than lemonade.

If one more person had water, it would be the same number as had orange.

Write one true and one false statement of your own.

Numeracy Focus 2: Games and Activity Support Sheets

98 Name ....

Numeracy Focus 2: Games and Activity Support Sheets

© P. Latham, H. Williams, M. Askew and S. Ebbutt 2001. Rigby
For copyright restrictions see reverse of title page.

99 Name ....

School dinners

Date ....

School dinner |

Packed lunch |

Go home |

Numeracy Focus 2: Games and Activity Support Sheets

100 Name ....

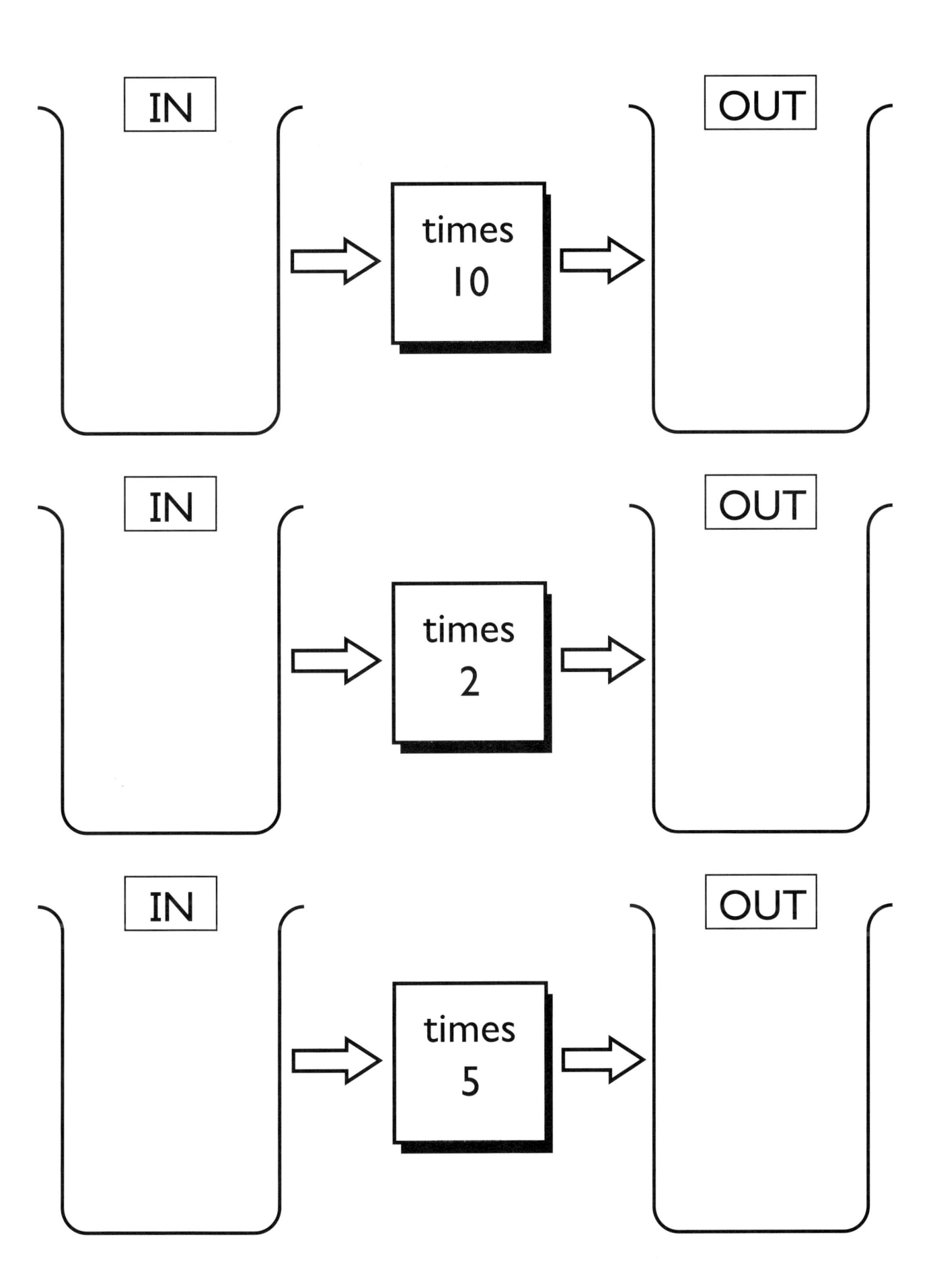

IN → times 10 → OUT

IN → times 2 → OUT

IN → times 5 → OUT

Numeracy Focus 2: Games and Activity Support Sheets

© P. Latham, H. Williams, M. Askew and S. Ebbutt 2001. Rigby
For copyright restrictions see reverse of title page.

101 Name

Numeracy Focus 2: Games and Activity Support Sheets

© P. Latham, H. Williams, M. Askew and S. Ebbutt 2001. Rigby
For copyright restrictions see reverse of title page.

102 Name

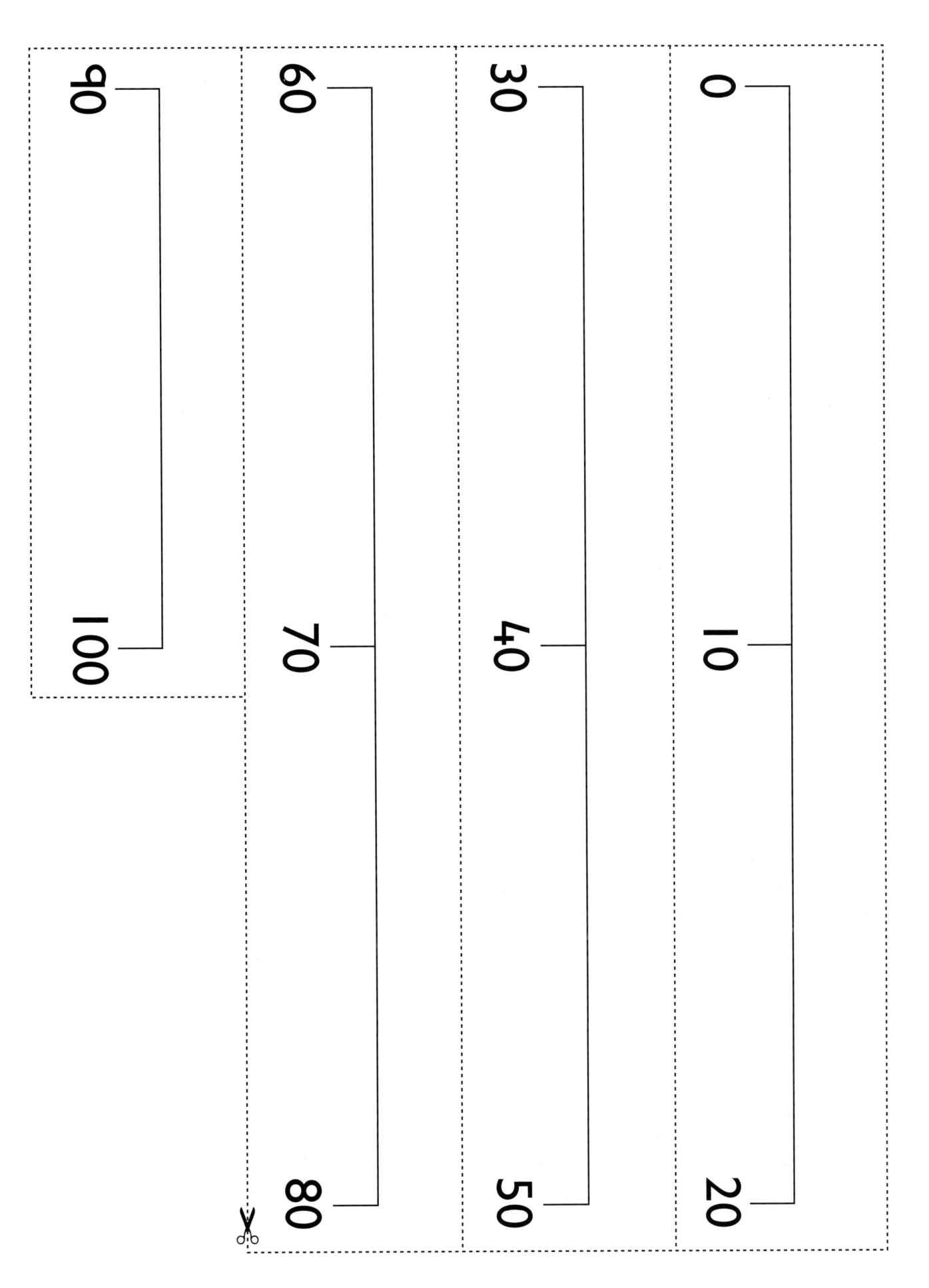

| 0 — 10 — 20 |
| 30 — 40 — 50 |
| 60 — 70 — 80 |
| 90 — 100 |

Numeracy Focus 2: Games and Activity Support Sheets

103 Name ....

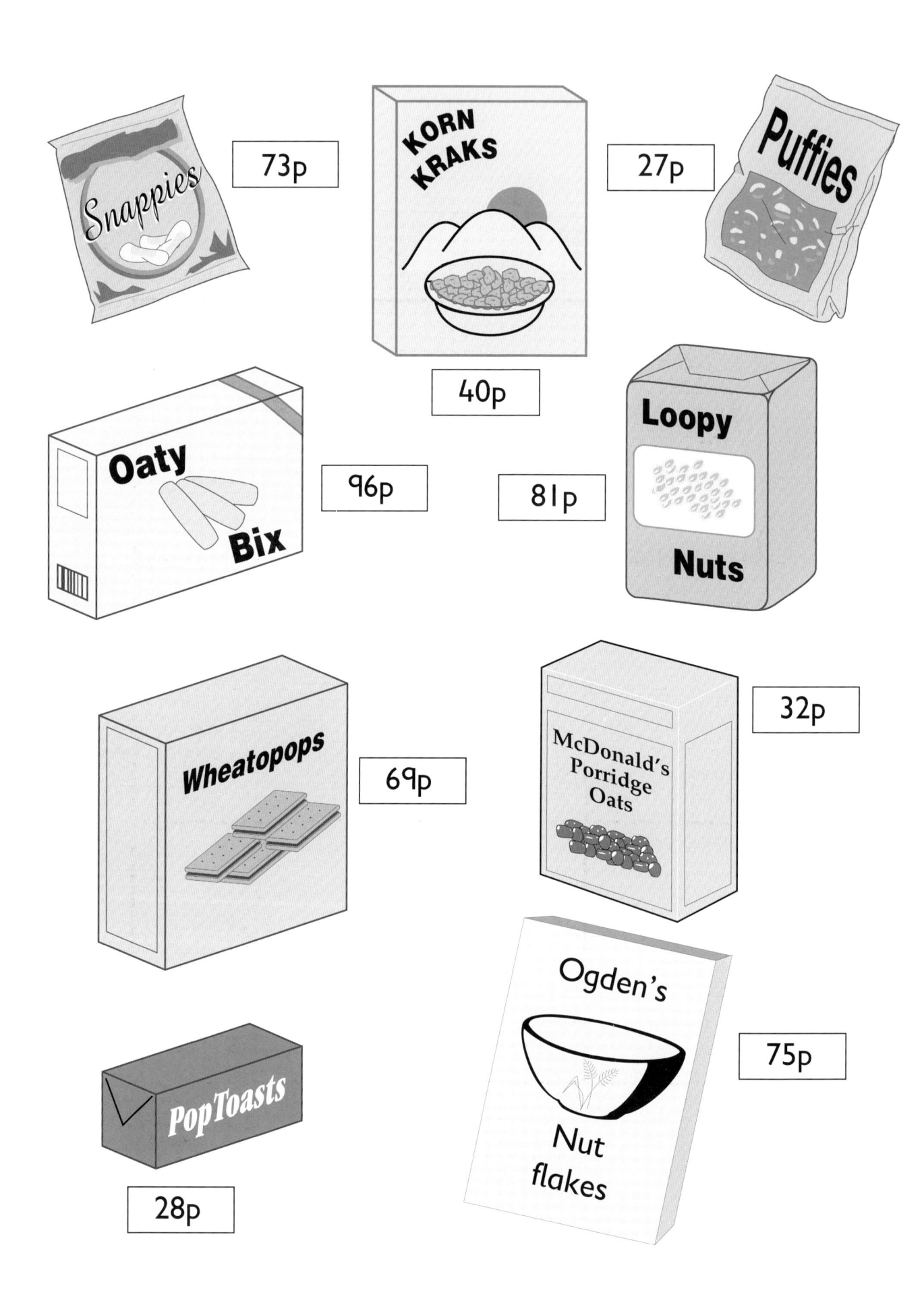

- Snappies — 73p
- KORN KRAKS — 40p
- Puffies — 27p
- Oaty Bix — 96p
- Loopy Nuts — 81p
- Wheatopops — 69p
- McDonald's Porridge Oats — 32p
- Ogden's Nut flakes — 75p
- PopToasts — 28p

Numeracy Focus 2: Games and Activity Support Sheets

104 Name ....

Numeracy Focus 2: Games and Activity Support Sheets

105 Names ....

Draw the level of water in the containers shown in the following pictures.

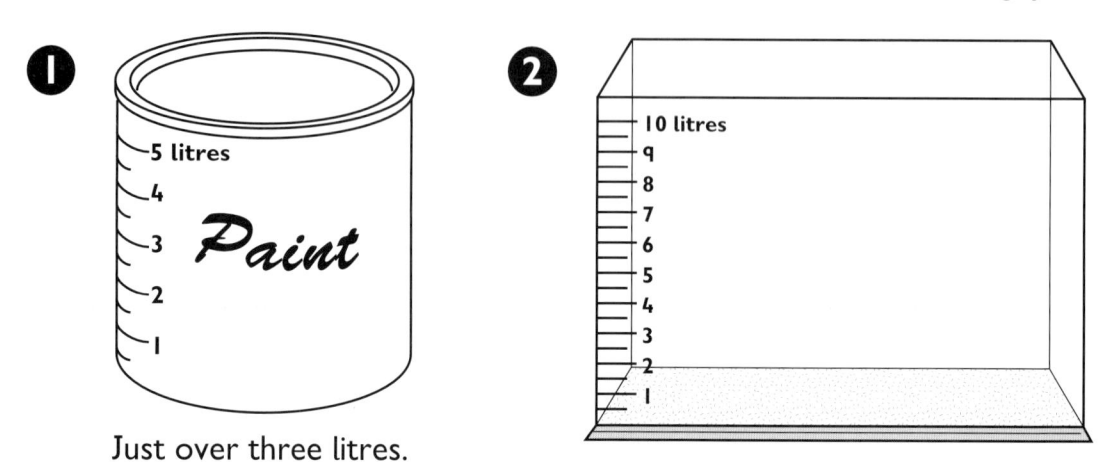

1

Just over three litres.

2

Exactly five-and-a-quarter litres.

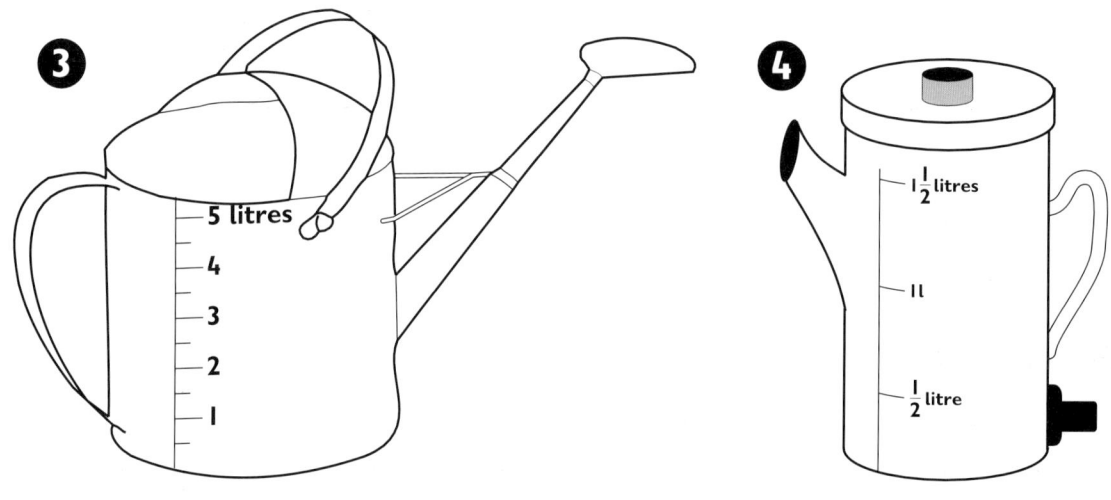

3

Exactly four-and-a-half litres.

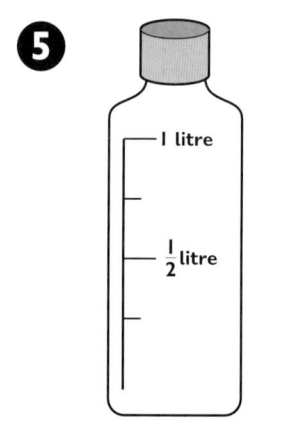

4

Just under one litre.

5

Nearly half a litre.

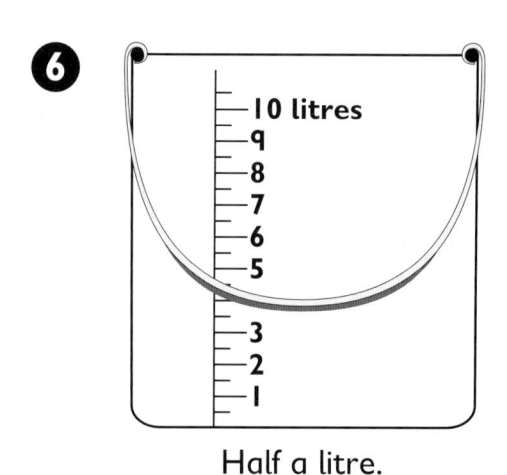

6

Half a litre.

Numeracy Focus 2: Games and Activity Support Sheets

106

107 Name ....

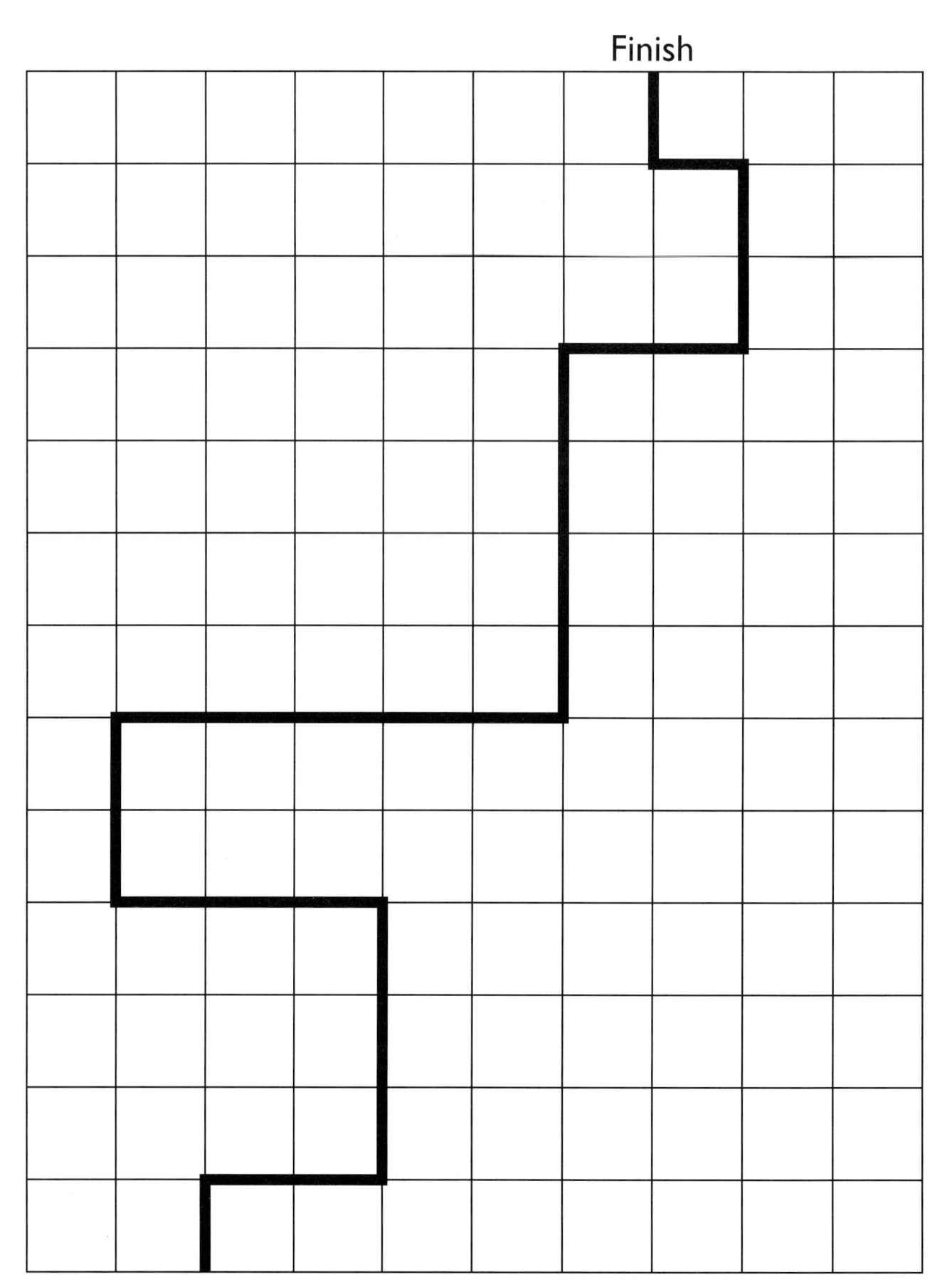

Finish

Start

Numeracy Focus 2: Games and Activity Support Sheets

© P. Latham, H. Williams, M. Askew and S. Ebbutt 2001. Rigby
For copyright restrictions see reverse of title page.

108 Name ....

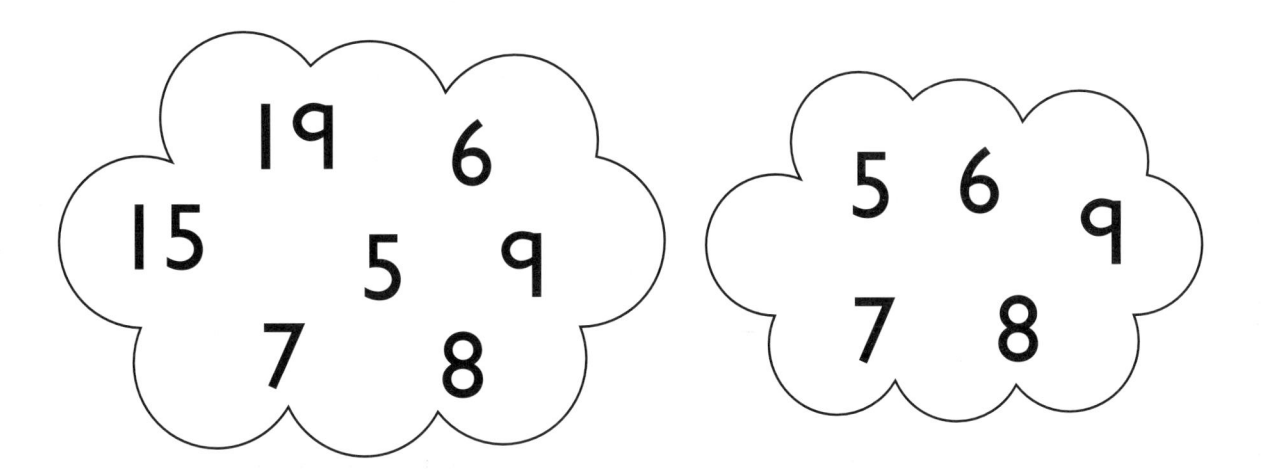

Cloud 1: 19, 15, 6, 5, 9, 7, 8

Cloud 2: 5, 6, 9, 7, 8

Write your calculations here:

Numeracy Focus 2: Games and Activity Support Sheets

Name ....

Example: 10p + 10p = 20p

1. 10p →[+10p] 20p →[ ] £1 →[ ] £1.20

2. 15p →[ ] 25p →[ ] 50p →[ ] £1

3. 20p →[ ] 30p →[ ] 50p →[ ] 90p

4. 20p →[ ] 50p →[ ] £1 →[ ] £2 →[ ] £2.20

Numeracy Focus 2: Games and Activity Support Sheets

6	2	9	3
3	8	1	4
9	5	2	7
7	1	4	8

8	12	20	10
18	6	4	14
16	8	2	18
10	14	12	4
6	2	8	20
10	4	6	16

112 Name ....

2	5	10	1
30	3	4	60
12	15	20	6
20	6	2	25
40	15	50	8
10	20	12	30

113 Name

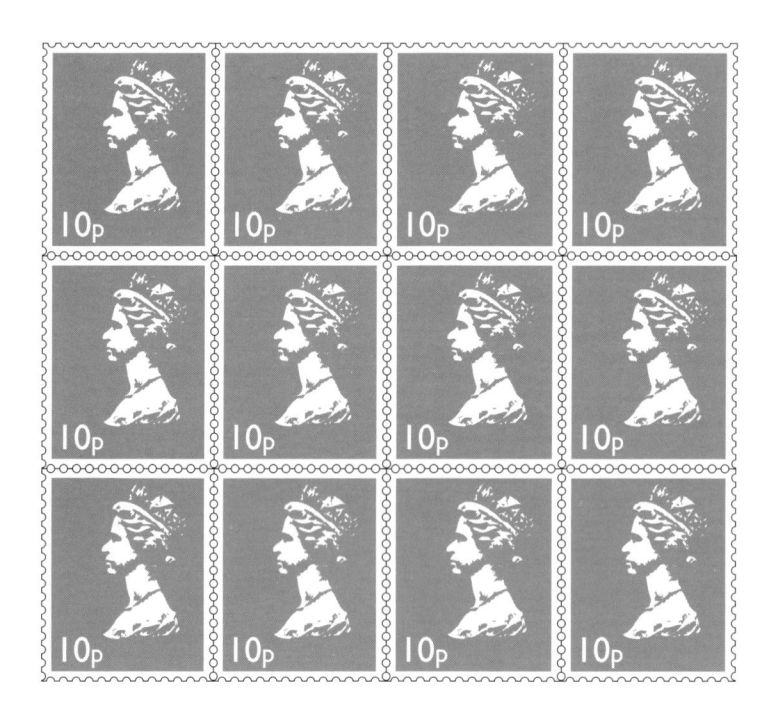

114 Name ....

8	14
16	10
12	20

Numeracy Focus 2: Games and Activity Support Sheets

© P. Latham, H. Williams, M. Askew and S. Ebbutt 2001. Rigby
For copyright restrictions see reverse of title page.

Choose a length of string and find one quarter of its length.

Choose a Plasticine ball and find one quarter of its mass.

Choose a container and fill it one quarter full.

116 Name

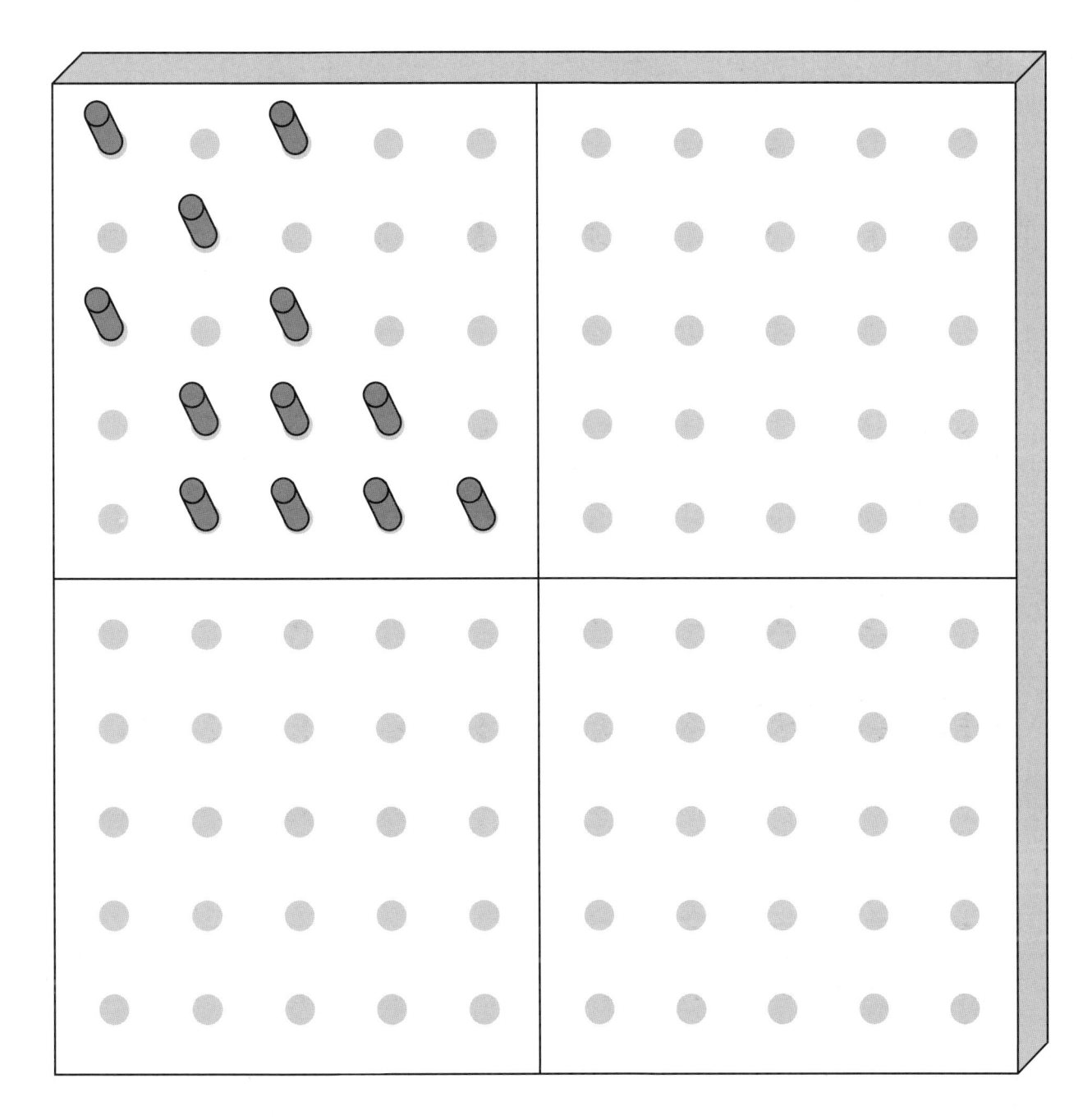

117 Name ....

Numeracy Focus 2: Games and Activity Support Sheets

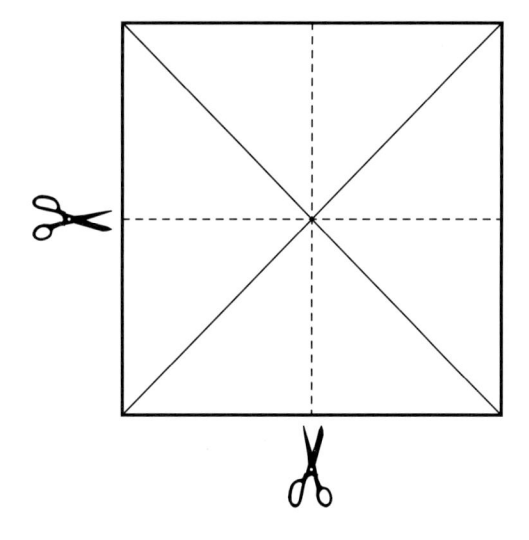

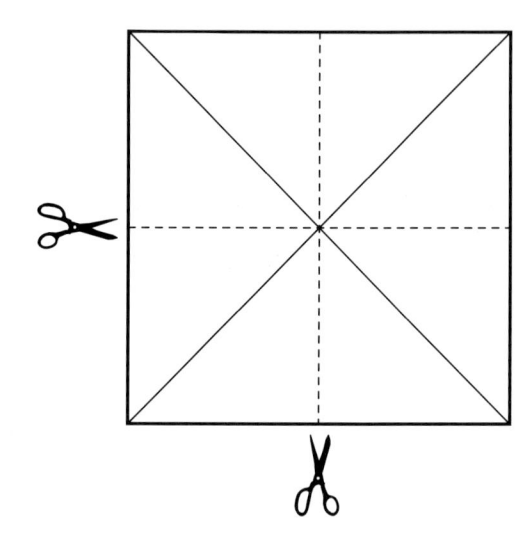

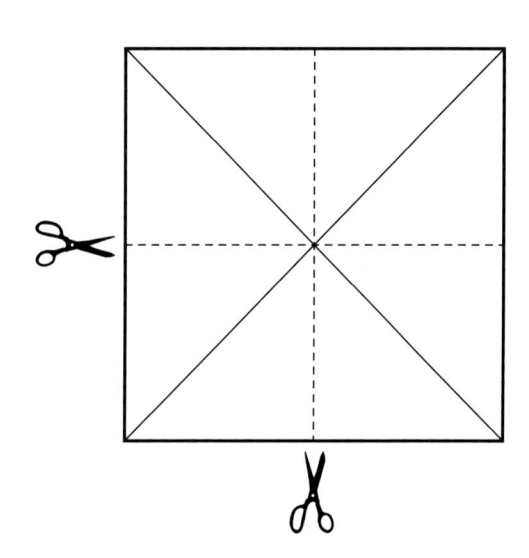

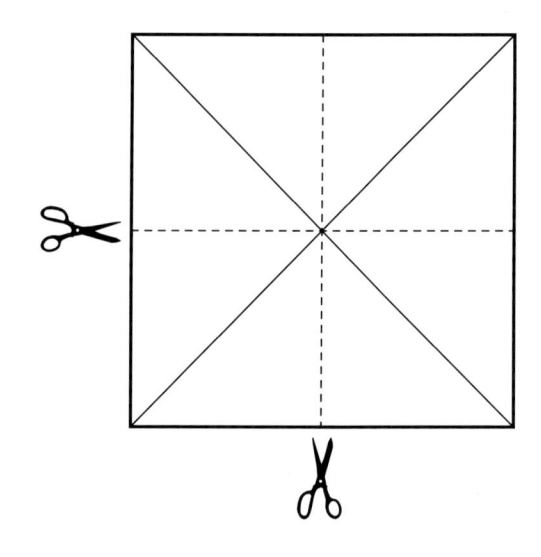

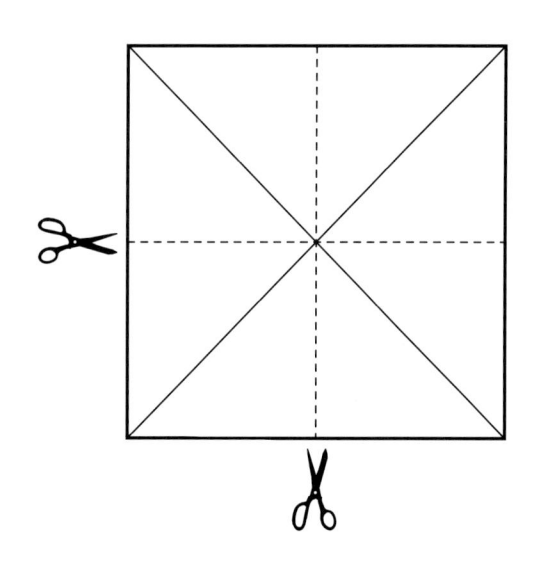

© P. Latham, H. Williams, M. Askew and S. Ebbutt 2001. Rigby
For copyright restrictions see reverse of title page.

118 Name ....

1 You need a jar lid, some Plasticine, scissors, paper or stickers for decoration and a glue stick.

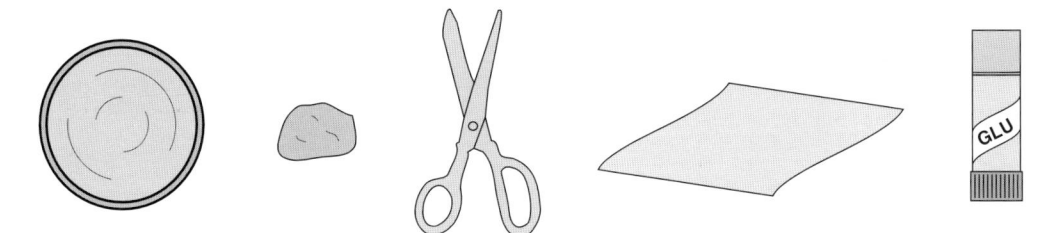

2 Working carefully, cut out two eyes, a mouth and a nose from the paper and stick them onto the lid to make a face.

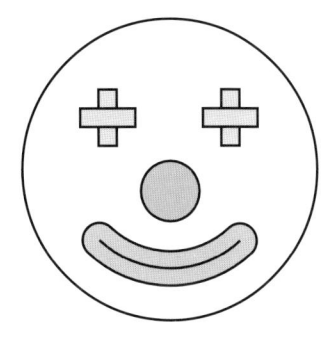

3 Roll the Plasticine into a sausage shape and smooth it around the bottom of the inside of the lid.

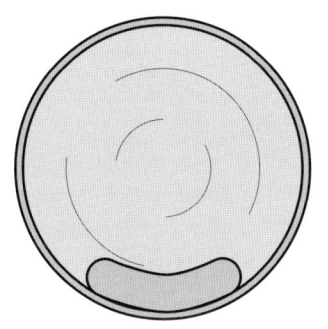

4 Rock the tocker from side to side – it should keep going by itself.

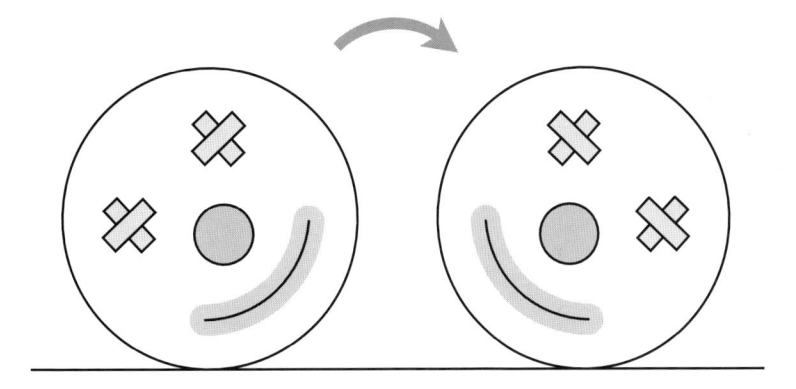

Numeracy Focus 2: Games and Activity Support Sheets

119

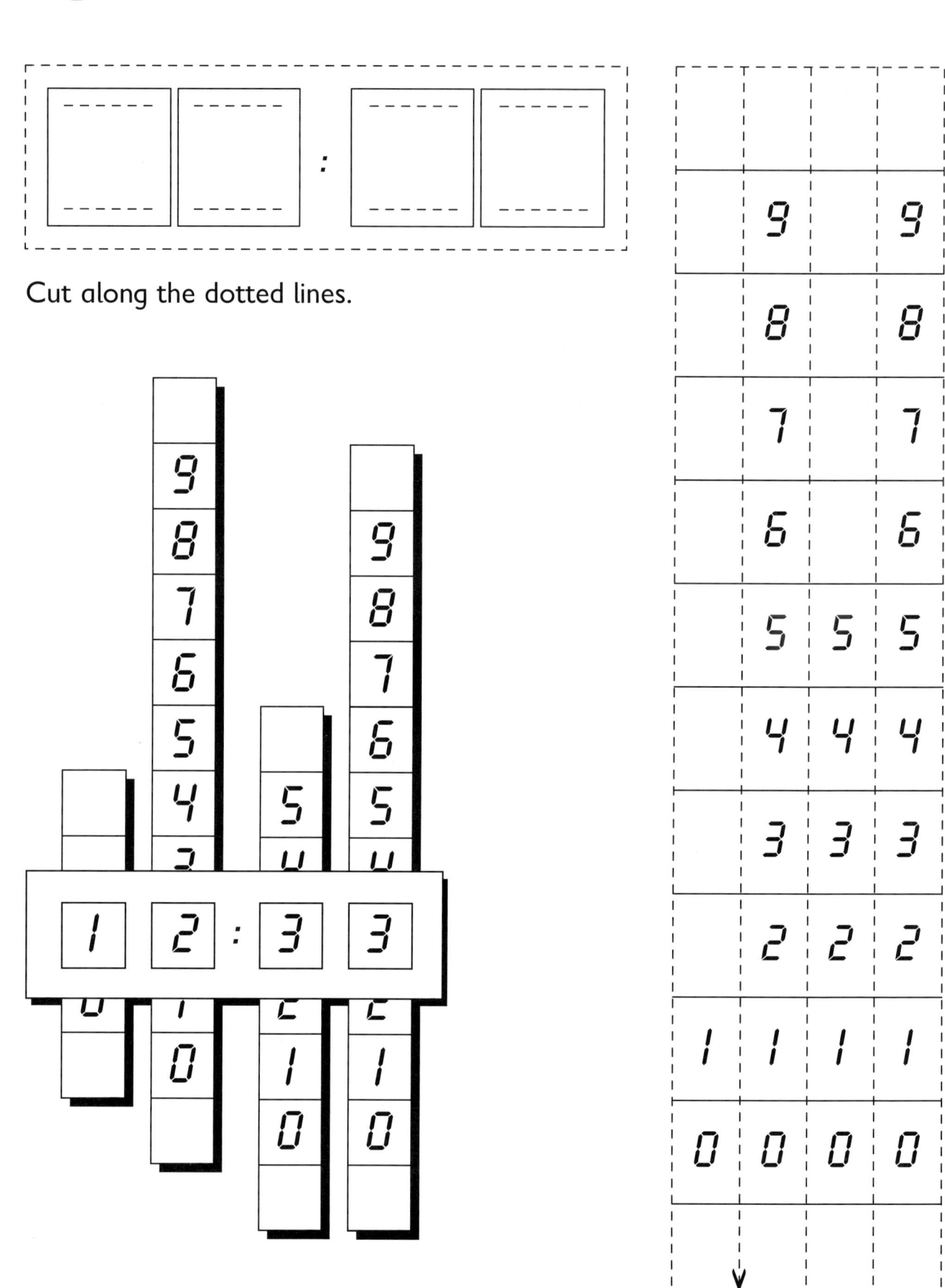

Cut along the dotted lines.

Cut out these strips and use them to make digital clock times.

Numeracy Focus 2: Games and Activity Support Sheets

© P. Latham, H. Williams, M. Askew and S. Ebbutt 2001. Rigby
For copyright restrictions see reverse of title page.

120

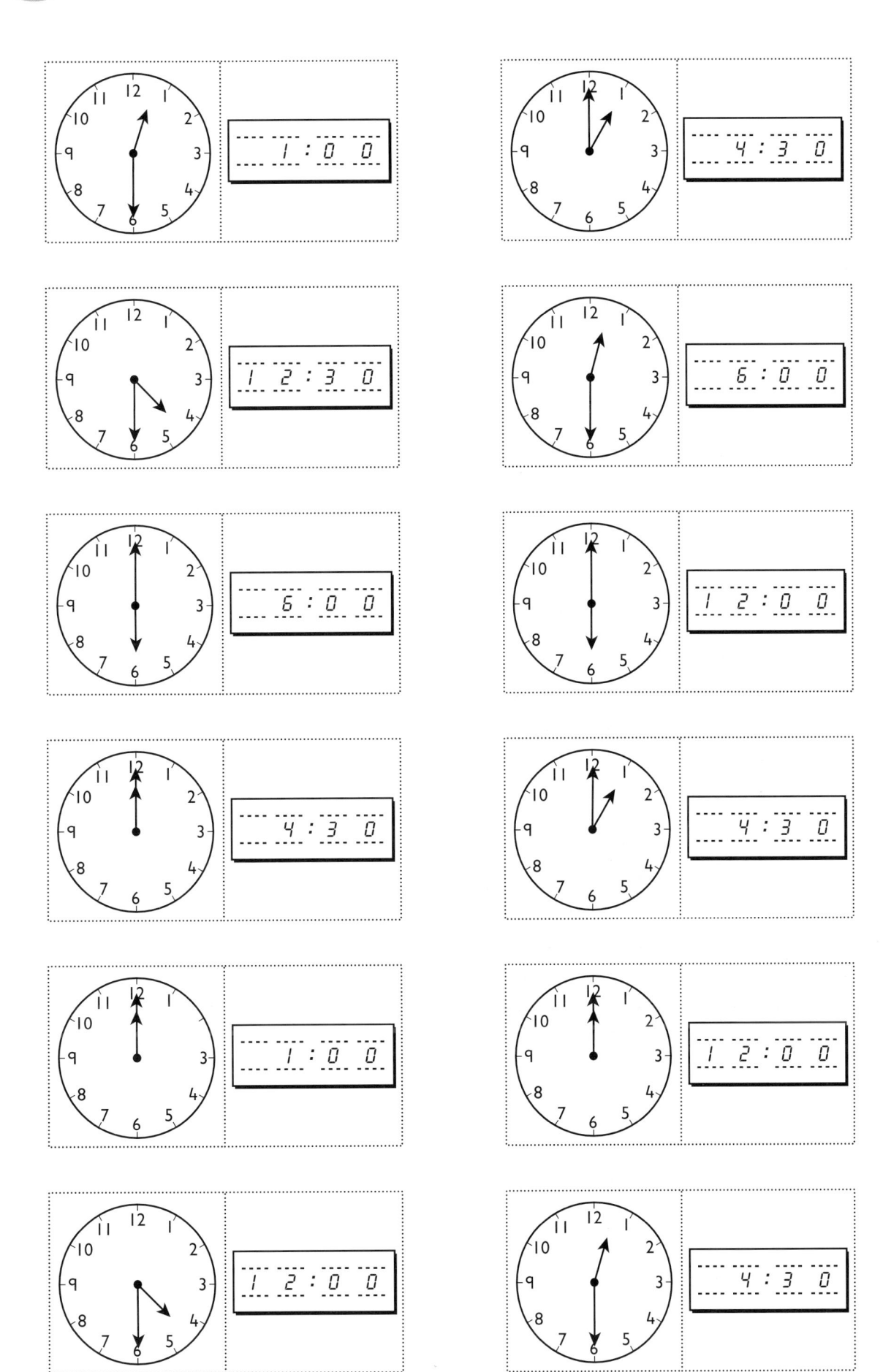

121

Clock	Time
1 o'clock	1:15
4:25	4:45
4:30	7:45
12:00	1:15
7:45	9:15
12:00	6:00
12:30	4:45

Numeracy Focus 2: Games and Activity Support Sheets

122 Name

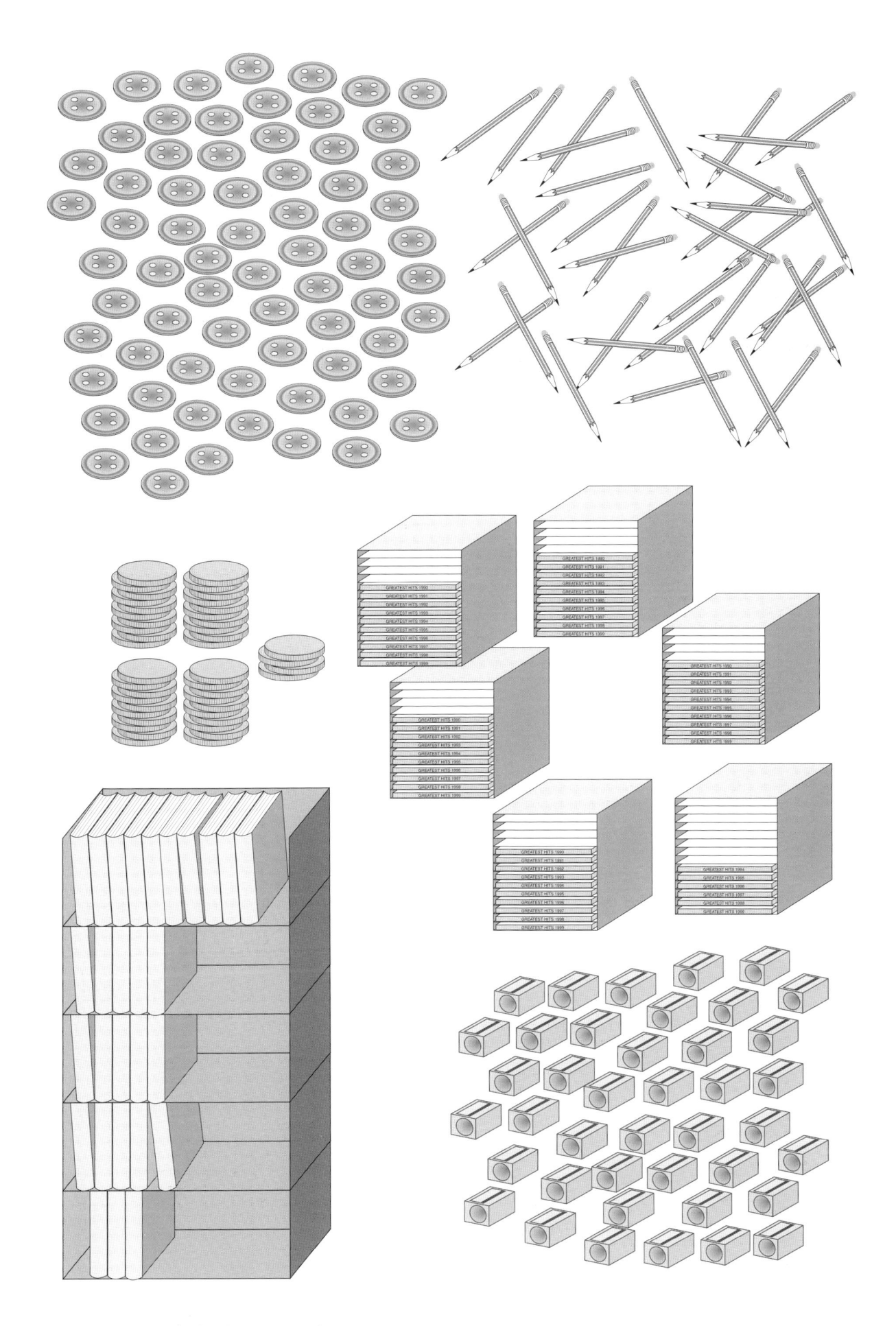

Numeracy Focus 2: Games and Activity Support Sheets

© P. Latham, H. Williams, M. Askew and S. Ebbutt 2001. Rigby
For copyright restrictions see reverse of title page.

123 Name ....

Peter Piper picked a peck of pickled pepper,
A peck of pickled pepper Peter Piper picked,
If Peter Piper picked a peck of pickled pepper,
Where's the peck of pickled pepper Peter Piper picked?

Letter	Tally	Total

124 Name ....

birds that you can see out of the window in 10 minutes
cars that pass the school in 10 minutes
coats on the pegs
chairs in the room
books on the shelf
people who walk along the corridor
lunch boxes
the number of times the teacher says 'the' in 10 minutes

Numeracy Focus 2: Games and Activity Support Sheets

21	22	23	24
25	26	27	28
29	30	31	32
33	34	35	36

Numeracy Focus 2: Games and Activity Support Sheets

37	38	39	40
41	42	43	44
45	46	47	48
49	50	51	52

53	54	55	56
57	58	59	60
<u>6</u>_<u>1</u>	62	63	64
65	<u>66</u>	67	<u>68</u>

69	70	71	72
73	74	75	76
77	78	79	80
81	82	83	84

129 Name

85	**86**	87	88
89	90	**91**	92
93	94	95	**96**
97	**98**	**99**	100

130

50	100
40	90
30	80
20	70
10	60

131 Name

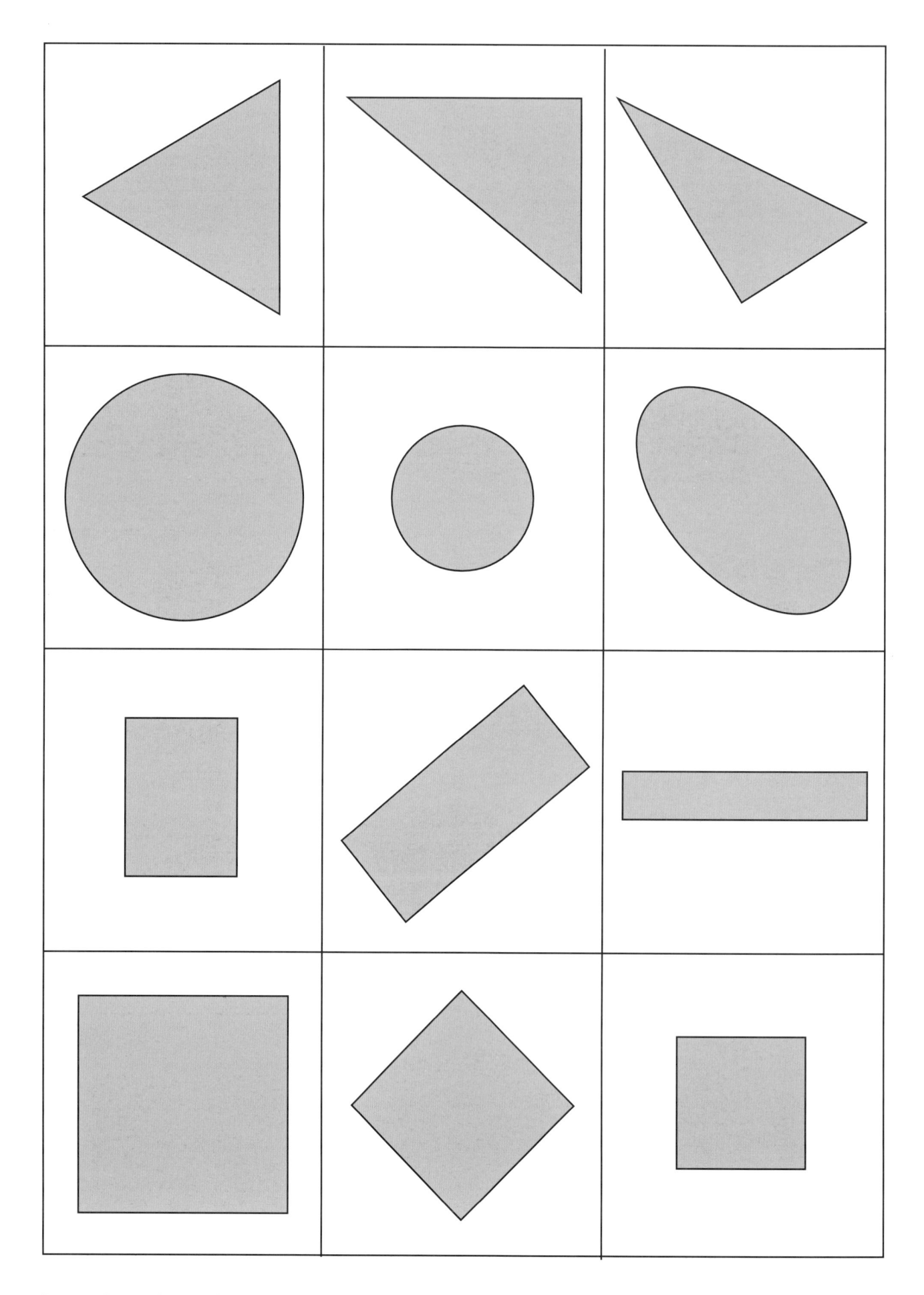

132 Name

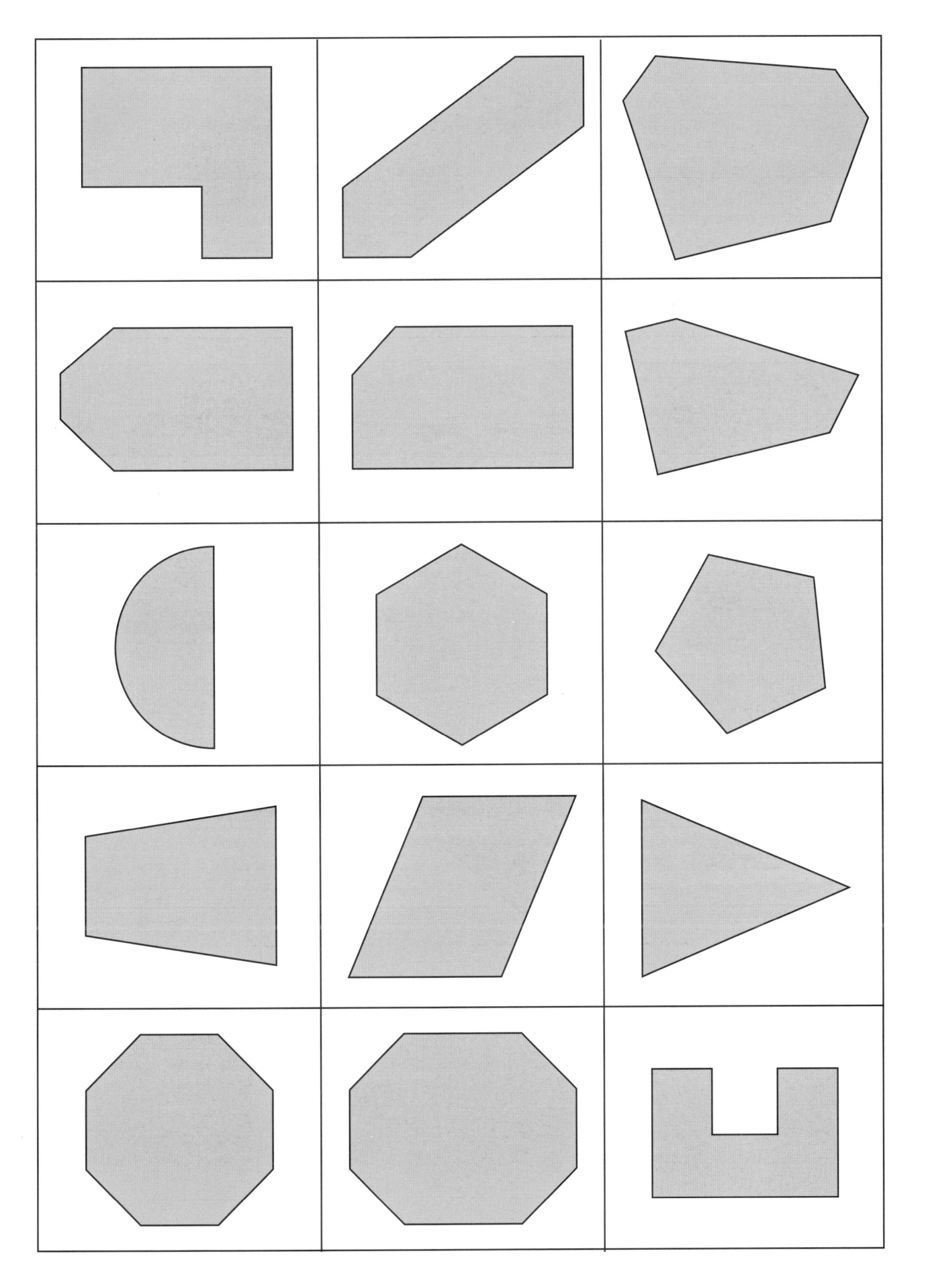

square	rectangle
circle	pentagon
hexagon	triangle
others	octagon

cube	cuboid
pyramid	sphere
cone	cylinder
others	

rectangle face	pentagon face	
square face	triangle face	hexagon face

Monday	Tuesday
Wednesday	Thursday
Friday	Saturday
Sunday	

long	short
longer	shorter
longest	shortest
metre	centimetre

heavy	light
heavier	lighter
heaviest	lightest
kilogram	gram

full	half full
empty	holds
contains	capacity
litre	millilitre

140 Name

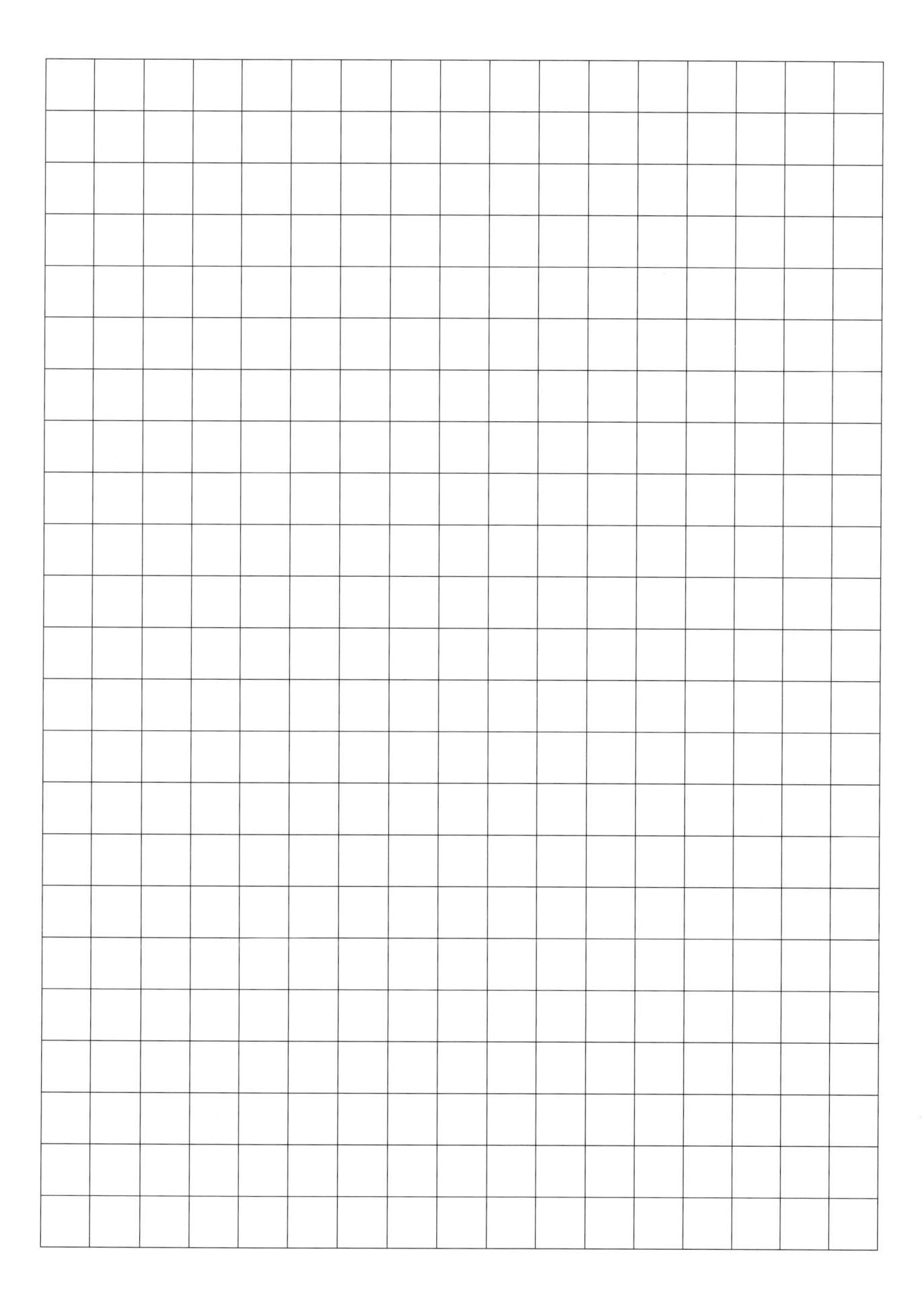

141 Name

summer	winter
spring	autumn

Numeracy Focus 2: Games and Activity Support Sheets